EMBRACING THE ABYSS

by John Smith

Copyright © 2017 by JOHN SMITH.

All rights reserved. This book or any portion thereof may not be reproduced or used in any manner whatsoever without the express written permission of the publisher except for the use of brief quotations in a book review.

Publishing Services provided by Paper Raven Books
Printed in the United States of America
First Printing, 2017

Hard copy ISBN: 978-0-9995170-0-0
Paperback ISBN: 978-0-9995170-1-7

TABLE OF CONTENTS

Prologue	i
Introduction	iii
The Abyss	xiii
Chapter 1	1
Chapter 2	5
Chapter 3	13
Chapter 4	23
Chapter 5	25
Chapter 6	31
Chapter 7	39
Chapter 8	43
Chapter 9	47
Chapter 10	51
Chapter 11	55
Chapter 12	63
Chapter 13	67
Chapter 14	81
Chapter 15	85
Chapter 16	89
Chapter 17	95
Chapter 18	101

Chapter 19	105
Chapter 20	109
Chapter 21	113
Chapter 22	119
Chapter 23	123
Chapter 24	129
Chapter 25	133
Chapter 26	137
Chapter 27	139
Chapter 28	145
Chapter 29	151
Chapter 30	153
Chapter 31	157
Chapter 32	163
Chapter 33	167
Appendix I	171
Appendix II	175
Appendix III	179
Appendix IV	185

PROLOGUE
The Boy

The boy was only three when he and his parents went to visit his grandparents, Pap and Mammy. They lived in the country in southern Kentucky where they were sharecroppers. On the first night at Pap and Mammy's place, the boy and his father fell asleep in the same bed. When his father got out of bed, the boy woke up. "Where you going, Daddy?"

"Going out to the barn to pee, Johnny. I'll be right back."

The boy fell into a deep sleep, comfortable in the knowledge that his Daddy would be there for him through the night.

When the boy awoke the next morning, he couldn't find either of his parents. Pap and Mammy broke the news that they had left for a short vacation, taking his baby sister with them. The boy was completely crushed and began crying. He sobbed harder and harder, uncontrollably, until he could barely catch his breath. Soon he was hysterical.

Pap and Mammy tried consoling the boy, even asking the boy's favorite uncle over to try and cheer him up. But to no avail. The boy had become inconsolable sobbing and stumbling, barely seeing through swollen eyes, the boy could not understand why his parents had left without him. Was he no longer loved?

The boy wasn't sleeping much, hardly any. His weeping and wailing were non-stop. Pap and Mammy begged for relief.

John Smith

His parents cut short their vacation after two days. They returned and rescued him.

Upon leaving Pap and Mammy's house, the boy began a long journey. A life sentence of figuring out what he had done wrong that had caused his parents to leave him behind.

INTRODUCTION
Opening Speech

My name really is John Smith. Three days from now I will stand in federal court before US District Judge Robert Maloney and be sentenced on a charge of fraud for my involvement as a high-ranking officer of Vernon Savings and Loan. I want to share with you how this happened to me so that you might remember, should it come close to happening to you; perish the thought.

In some respects, as I look back, I still don't believe it. But I live with it every day. I don't have any other choice. How could I have been so stupid?

This is not a story about your small-town banker that dips into the cash drawer every now and then for himself or his girlfriend. It's not a story about the guy who worked in the back room and had never been promoted, the guy who was mad at his boss—mad at the whole world—who thought he deserved a self-reward by socking away a little cash every chance he got.

Savings and loans (S&Ls) at the beginning of the 1980s were a struggling industry. They were not the same as banks, because they were primarily limited to making loans for home ownership. The model worked by offering low interest rates on long-term mortgage loans. Prospective home owners who couldn't afford a loan from a regular bank could come to an S&L and get a cheaper mortgage. But by the early 1980s, the financial playing field was changing. Interest rates had risen to double digits, meaning S&Ls had to pay depositors more for their funds. This left S&Ls in the impossible situation of paying double digits on deposits, while offering only single digits on home loans.

Federal regulators were searching for a solution to this problem. They began looking at real estate entrepreneurs. The real estate industry in Texas had been successful. After all, real estate developers with large balance sheets, appeared to know what they were doing, and they had significant experience with real estate loans.

The regulators' theory was that if these real estate entrepreneurs were able to borrow money, then they ought to be able to lend money. So, the federal regulations for savings and loans were changed to allow ownership of S&Ls by real estate developers and entrepreneurs, after their state commissioners reviewed and approved the transaction.

This loosening of the reins, or deregulation, brought the entrepreneurs aboard, and it worked for a while. But within two to three years, the plan went awry, primarily because of greed leading to fraud. The regulators' decision to deregulate would ultimately produce a moral hazard and what's known as zombie financial institutions. There was stupidity, yes on my part, too, but also a lack of awareness and consciousness, snuffed out by a plethora of pretense and a deluge of denial.

Embracing The Abyss

I consider myself a regular guy. I was born in Nashville, Tennessee to God-loving parents from the country in Tennessee and Kentucky. I grew up some in Oklahoma City and then moved when I was a high school sophomore to Dallas, Texas.

In 1965, the summer before my senior year, my friend's dad got us jobs at the Texas school book depository warehouse. In case you don't remember, in November 1963, JFK was shot by Lee Harvey Oswald from a sixth-floor window of the Texas school book depository office building.

Our work in the warehouse consisted of packing boxes of textbooks to be sent to various school districts across Texas. One day, I was given the task of delivering an envelope to an office in the TSBD building where the shooting had occurred.

After delivering the item, I thought I might have a look around and took the freight elevator upstairs to the sixth floor. There were no barriers or cautions or warnings that would have prevented me from exploring, so I proceeded to the corner of the large room, to the window where Lee Harvey Oswald sat and waited.

I must say it was a bit spooky. From the looks of it, that corner of the room was left the way it was found. I remember seeing chicken bones and assumed that Lee Harvey Oswald had had something to eat while waiting on JFK's limousine to pass by. In front of the window was a desk that he probably used to aim his rifle. For some fun, I decided to put a chair on top of the desk. Discovering a round, three-foot-long piece of wood, I picked it up and put it across my lap as I sat in the chair on top of the desk in front of the window.

There were tourists outside on the grassy knoll, and it wasn't but a few minutes before I was noticed by a crowd gathering below. As the crowd began to grow, many of them started pointing toward me. I realized I needed to get my ass out of there. Without delay, I was in the elevator having a downward ride, goose bumps covering both of my arms.

When I got back to the warehouse, my friends asked me how it went. I told them about the chair on the desk. They got a big kick out of that, and I guess I did, too.

When I graduated from high school, I assumed I knew everything there was to know about college. I had finished with the TSBD and was now working 50 hours a week at Collins Radio, a large manufacturer of electronic devices for the Vietnam War. I knew then that the most important thing to me was the '66 GTO convertible that I had, so I decided that I was going to get into college and get out with the least amount of trouble.

My first semester, I signed up for 21 hours of classes, plus a lab , but tried carrying that only on Mondays, Wednesdays, and Fridays so I could continue working and making money. I think I made it past Halloween, but I'm not real sure. That time in my life was somewhat of a blur as I lived it. The one thing I do know is that after I dropped out of college in the fall of 1966, only a few months from starting, I got to work more hours at Collins Radio.

The draft lottery was in effect, and I probably watched too many John Wayne movies, because even though I enjoyed working at Collins Radio, I volunteered to go into the army. I wanted to go to Vietnam, and I did. I am a decorated veteran of Vietnam. When I returned to the States after Nam, I became a "teacher" in the army. I smile when I write that, because what I mean by teacher is that I was a drill sergeant. You know, the soldiers with the Smokey the Bear hats? Hey, don't knock it; I was the honor graduate of my drill sergeant school!

After my discharge from the army, I returned to Denton, Texas wanting another chance at college. I didn't know what I wanted to study, but I knew I wanted a college degree. I married my first wife only three days after departing the army, and we had twin sons born during my first fall semester. The G.I. Bill and three or four part-time jobs supported us. I never knew how important $210 a month was until then.

Now, it's almost as though I'm reliving that prospect of poverty again. Not much is left over these days after the legal fees are paid.

When I was a college student my second go around, I became the Attorney General of the Student Government Association. I was the guy who interpreted the rules and matters of "law." I was the one with the big paddle that spent the meetings at the back of the room as the sergeant at arms.

It was my senior year, and I still hadn't chosen a major. I had completed almost all the hours necessary in the school of business, but hadn't chosen a specific business major. The time had come. I could put it off no longer. I recall going around to the different departmental offices stopping in to visit, asking them why I should choose their department for my major.

One Saturday morning, I walked into the Department of Accounting office and met a man named Herschel Anderson. I didn't know him from Adam but I soon found out that Dr. Herschel Anderson was a man of quick wit with a large desire to help others.

I don't know how he did it so early in the morning, but he had one of those great big cigars in his mouth, and he could talk at the same time, too. He asked if I had taken accounting yet. I answered yes.

"Both Accounting I and II?"

I again said yes.

"What were your grades?"

I replied, "As."

"Both I and II?"

"Yes."

He paused, his head dropping as he looked through the floor. I was somewhat startled when all of a sudden, he looked at me with utter frustration and confusion, like I was crazy. He said, "Are you kidding me? What is wrong with you boy? Accounting is your ticket to the big show. You can't do any better than accounting. You can't make As in accounting and walk away from it!" His voice grew louder and louder. "This is the bus you want to be on! If you think about all that stuff the other departments offer, you know they're nuts. They get part-time jobs. You're done with those other departments!"

In that span of ten minutes or so, Herschel made his message clear to me. "If you do this, then from this you can do anything else. You can do all that other stuff when you want to. If you choose that other stuff now, you're going to have a tough time with this road if you change your mind." Herschel was candid, and his message poured from his heart straight into mine.

Of course, I'm glad now for what he said. I believed him then, and I believe it now. I was one lucky guy to have stumbled into Dr. Anderson that Saturday morning, big cigar and all.

I maintained a 4.0 GPA, and graduated magna cum laude with a degree in accounting. I got into an argument with the people in administration about why I shouldn't have been classified summa cum laude, the higher honor, for my 4.0. They reminded me of the four deadly withdrawal/failings I'd had my first time at college. Surprised, I said, "Oh, those still count?" Well, shut my mouth.

When the recruiters came to campus, I interviewed and received offers of employment, but I accepted the one that I thought would be able to provide the best post-college education. I chose Alford Meroney & Co, the largest regional public accounting firm in the southwest.

I spent five years at Alford Meroney & Co (AM & Co) and feel fortunate that I got the education I wanted. With them, I was able to work with a variety of clients in a variety of businesses, large and small. I dealt with audits, all types of taxation, including individual, corporate, and estate planning projections. I was also involved with the computer services department, also known as management information services.

It was almost too good to be true. I believed I was being prepared for something more important, possibly a career requiring collective experience for advancement and success.

For most of my life, when my head was on right, my intuition provided a flow of information that kept challenging what I thought I could be and what I ultimately would be. My mindset was usually geared for success, and I spent most of my waking minutes analyzing how to make these thoughts become reality.

I enjoyed public accounting. At AM & Co, there was a great deal of camaraderie, respect for each other, and good friendship. I received the professional education I sought. I realized that your college education is your foundation. The critical part of learning takes place out there in the real world, but you can't get there unless you go through basic training in college. Funny how that works.

After five years of public accounting, I committed the ultimate sin: I went to work for a client for bigger money. I learned a lot about closely-owned family businesses. Namely, if you find yourself on the wrong side of the family that controls the business, you're going to be history sooner than later. After working five years straight in public accounting, in the ensuing two years, I had four jobs.

Finally, I found a job with Dondi, a startup construction-development firm. I felt lucky. Dondi had plans to build condos in the Dallas-Fort Worth (DFW) area, Louisiana, and Florida. I recall thinking that this was a company where things were going to be done right. I worked hard; I'd been given a new opportunity in something I knew about, which was real estate with taxation, partnerships, and corporate reporting. These are the things that I had cut my teeth on in public accounting. I was counting on taking a large step upward after proving my capabilities. I felt confident that I could do this, even though uncertainty often interrupted my thought process of a real world education.

But the real lessons I would learn weren't the ones I was expecting. Those came only through the Abyss.

THE ABYSS

Being a part of your soul, the Abyss is not something you recognize right away. It's a part of you that you don't come in touch with very often. It seems unreachable at first, until you feel its presence and know it's you. It resides in the area inside you that's parked a ways away in a safe place, resting under a Do Not Disturb sign.

This is your own sacred ground for times when you reach the point where you can no longer answer to yourself, when you've exhausted all efforts at rationalization. This is the time when you need something deep from within, something strong to support yourself. It's the place where you engage in the ultimate struggle for truth, where you're aching for a lasting answer.

Often, in an attempt to expedite things, you may be able to disguise the true answer, the real answer, by fooling yourself with a quick, fleeting fix. You do this because you are trying to protect the image of you, the one you have of yourself. You are trying to protect your self-image: the unstained version of yourself that you still covet and caress.

If you have not recently traveled into and through your soul for a visit, know that the Abyss, as gatekeeper, may not notice you at first. You identify with and respond to karma at the Abyss. Your depth and breadth of consciousness increases, leading to a greater awareness that protects you.

John Smith

    Sincerely bestow the breath from deep within you; grasp the abyss, embrace it, and hold on for dear life.

CHAPTER 1
The On-Deck Circle

Dallas, Texas, October 13, 1988

Couldn't complain about the weather. It was in the mid-70s and not much wind for an October day in Dallas. I was supposed to meet my attorney and friend, Steve Brutsché, at the Justice Department office on the third floor of the Earle Cabell Federal Building downtown. He had wanted to talk with the Justice Department attorneys in person before the judge passed sentence on me, but they turned us down. Our last hour appeal to them, to hopefully soften their view of my receiving time behind bars, went unheard.

The atmosphere was highly charged regarding savings and loans and anyone involved with the industry. Federal task forces in Texas had been formed with a vengeance to bring to justice members of the S&L industry not only for engaging in illegal lending practices, but also in retaliation for S&L owners seeking help from politicians who attempted to strong arm regulators and federal law enforcement. With my case being one of the first to be tried, we knew they were out for blood and headlines, as big as they could get them.

We rode the elevator to the 16th floor where the hallways leading to the judges' courtrooms and chambers all looked alike. Clearing the U. S. Marshal's security checkpoint allowed us access to the sterile hallways, walls of federal marble flanking each step. The light grey paint added to the bleakness and to the difficulty of finding reference points as we made our way. Not saying much as we walked, I began to think that the monotony of the décor would eventually cause us to get lost, and I feared I would start to panic. I'm not a fast walker, so it wasn't easy keeping up with Steve's loping strides. Covering the ground quickly, more quickly than I would have liked, we approached the judge's courtroom. And my destiny.

Steve asked if my wife, Alex, and my sons were already in the courtroom and if Coach, my best friend, was ready to go.

I mumbled a tongue twisted, "Yes, I think so."

We opened the large double doors, trimmed with brass and covered with fingerprints left by those who had entered before us. We stepped into the courtroom and it seemed cavernous. I felt so little as I walked toward the monstrous circumstances waiting ahead, wondering if I would walk out of there with or without handcuffs. The vibrations behind the big doors were thick and heavy, feeling like low rolling thunder rumbling nearby. My heart was pounding like a movie drumroll just prior to hearing the words: ready, aim, fire. The scene was serene and surreal. My life would soon be decided, whether in my favor or not. The tense feeling along my arms stretched tight toward my neck and shoulders.

Marching toward our designated seats, my practiced focus, as a government witness during the past eight months, was to look straight ahead to the tables where the Justice

Department lawyers and FBI agents would sit. As we passed the full rows of reporters and spectators, I could feel the presence of those sitting quietly in their designated area to my right, both those who had come to show their support, and those who had come to see... but let's not think about that now.

Although the courtroom was only about 60 by 40 feet, it felt enormous. Like the time I was five years old, when I caught my hand in the teeth of an outdoor clothes ringer at the top of the Russells' backyard in Nashville. As I ran screaming down the hill, leaving a kid-sized trail of blood behind me, help at their house just 40 yards or so below seemed a mile away.

Drawing my attention to the swinging doors in the low wooden wall that separated the audience from the actors, Steve warned, "Be careful when we're called up to not let them swing after you go through. It's considered a sign of disrespect." I began to imagine my holding them for a small eternity, just to make sure they were quiet. We took our seats in the front row of the audience and waited.

"All rise," came the call, as Judge Robert Maloney entered the courtroom. I wondered if the entrance of another warm body might bring a warmer feeling into the courtroom, but I had my doubts. It felt like a tomb, where alabaster sconces met pallid, judiciary marble, paired with pale grey paint, cold and aseptic. The wood paneled walls were not enough to make the morgue-like setting any more comfortable, nor was the judge.

The judge took his seat, followed by the rest of us. The clerk began to read the case of a man not too much younger than me, who was apprehended for selling meth. After dispensing a pound or two of pointed criticism, the judge then declared, "I hereby sentence you to 78 months' custody of the Bureau of Prisons."

Stealthily, two U.S. Marshals had appeared out of nowhere—maybe from the cracks in the wood paneling. They were standing directly behind the man a micro-second before the judge had said, "78."

The purpose of the immediate presence of the U.S. Marshals seemed twofold. One, to scare the bajeebers out of everyone looking on, and two, to keep the man from bolting from the courtroom in case he didn't like the sentence the judge handed him.

The marshals quickly handcuffed him and led him to the rear of the courtroom, through a door in the corner that looked about the size of the rabbit hole Alice fell into. I imagined it led to another maze of ubiquitous hallway hell, onto prisoner processing, and then to federal prison. I somehow maintained my composure throughout all of this, although I don't recall breathing much.

Then it hit me. *I'm up next.*

CHAPTER 2
The Looking Glass Window

After college, I spent five years with AM & Co in Dallas, doing public accounting. After that, I bounced around between three or four jobs within a two-year period; what a blur. I knew that I needed to find something stable and soon, before my resume began playing merry-go-round music to accompany its already amusement-park-like appearance. I could have kicked myself for leaving AM & Co, just as it was merging with Arthur Young, but the siren's sound of opportunity had commandeered my decision making for better or worse.

It turned out that the different companies I worked for after leaving AM & Co all had their problems, be it questionable business practices or power struggles among family members.

In retrospect, I realize I didn't ask the right questions when making the decision to work for each of these companies. Asking the right questions, and not just the questions that bring the right answers, is something I'd later learn is imperative. Case in point: not long after I accepted my fourth job, I learned that the payroll taxes had not been paid to the IRS in more than four months. This, of course, meant that a serious situation was underway, a situation that was usually non-recoverable. So, it wasn't very long until the decision was made to shut the business down via bankruptcy. On a Friday afternoon, I sat down with the four-packs-a-day treasurer and the single owner (his business partner had recently skedaddled for higher ground), and we went over the plan. Next door stood all the employees who would not only be told they no longer had jobs, but they would also learn that there wasn't a pay check for the week they had just worked. As we sat together, waiting for the crowd to gather in the next room, the owner and treasurer wrung their hands so much I thought the age spots would rub off. After checking our watches a couple of hundred times, it was time for us to do what we had to do.

Just as we were about to open the door and join the waiting employees, the owner placed his hand against the door, looked at me, and said, "I can't do this, John Boy. You'll have to tell them."

With the three of us wedged against the door, I knew there was no chance of going back into the office to talk it over. So, I swallowed hard, nodded okay, and then followed them into the large, crowded room.

As we positioned for space and waited for quiet, I thought, "I'm okay. I'm not the one needing rescue," and took a deep breath. Listening for guidance, contemplating the right words, I drew from my drill sergeant training and anchored my feet to the shiny shop floor, knowing that what I was about to say would be devastating. I felt a presence had joined us, bringing me inner strength to say what I had to say. Without visibly shaking, I gave the news to looks of disbelief, disappearing hope, and the onset of despair. My words were clear and on target, as though they had been fired from a stun gun.

I was the only employee to stay on and continue to guide the company through bankruptcy. The process did not take as long as you might think. After a month, the work I was doing for the bankruptcy trustee was coming to an end. I would soon be out of work again, and I had started to despair that I would ever find something stable and secure. To keep the panic at bay, I meditated more than usual. I'd first learned and started meditating when I began joint marital therapy, and continued with Dr. Brown, a Dallas clinical psychologist. I found it helpful when dealing with stress. Achieving mindfulness during meditation is a valuable skill to have: it's about preparation for a calm mental state. And you never know when that skill is going to be needed.

***

It was July 1980 on a Monday, and man was it hot. Over the weekend, I had attended an outdoor wedding. "Stupid is, as stupid does," Forest Gump would say, for getting married outside on a July day in Dallas. My wedding present for the bride and groom was a jumbo outdoor thermometer, which pointed to 113 degrees as we'd stood in the shade of some small trees, where those of us crazy enough to be there had gathered to wilt. With such a hot weekend, it was no surprise that today was supposed to be another scorcher, and only a little before 1:00 p.m., my car's AC was having trouble keeping up as I drove to a North Dallas office for an interview.

Unexpectedly, a friend of a friend had suggested my name for an interview to the president of Dondi Group, a startup construction and development company with new offices in North Dallas. They were gearing up to build multiple condominium complexes, and I was headed their way on this roasting hot day to see if I was a fit to be their financial guy. As I drove north, thankful for this opportunity, I wondered what God really looked like. All my years of going to church gave me ample views of pictures of Jesus, but I don't recall seeing any pictures of God. Not one. The Bible says God appeared as a burning bush and spoke to Moses. A burning bush was perfect for a hot day like that. I had a really good feeling about this interview and if I was going to give thanks, I just wanted to know what God looks like. A burning bush would have to do, I was almost there. Thanks, God!

I parked my hail damaged, seven-year-old Toyota at the end of the two-story office building, in front of a large window facing the service road. I stepped out of my trusty vehicle (Well, lame AC but I got there, didn't I?), tightened up my tie, pulled the wet part of my shirt away from my back, and put on my suit coat. I stood very still, saying hopeful words toward my forthcoming fate, as I placed my hands on the Corolla's roof. I yelled and jerked my hands away from the searing top to keep them from melting. I clasped them against my chest, looked up, and asked again for assistance from the man upstairs. I needed this job something bad.

I left my car smoldering in front of a large window and made my way through the entrance doors, into a partially furnished reception area. I said hello to the executive secretary, declined her offer of coffee—wasn't it hot enough already?—and sat on the small sofa.

I silently repeated my mantra (a personal word that brings calm), nervously running my fingers around my neck where it met my shirt collar, wondering if it was the occasion or the heat, or both.

After a few minutes, I was escorted to the president's office and met Rick Ramsey. As I entered and shook his hand, I realized his sizable desk overlooked a large window onto a '73 Toyota Corolla that looked a lot like mine. Embarrassment washed over me as I figured he had more than likely sat and watched my clasped-handed plea to the man above.

Rickie Wayne Ramsey was about six foot one, maybe six two, a rugged-looking guy with dark hair. He had paid a heavy price for the ruggedness, having had his face rebuilt after a tree-hanging trip-wire explosive said good morning one day to him in Nam. After having watched too many John Wayne movies—his namesake—he had insisted on being the point man of every patrol for his marine infantry squad, even though he was oversized for the job. For his gung ho initiative, he was awarded two and a half years in various military hospitals, where they put his face back together, piece by piece.

I liked Rick. He had at one time been the controller-chief financial officer of the home building company, Raldon. So, he knew the drill and what he wanted: discipline, dedication, someone versatile who could be quick on their feet. You see, bean counters are the first butts of jokes in the business world, especially in the construction industry.

During the interview, Rick and I learned we had a lot in common—Nam, both CPAs, putting ourselves through college, and both Church of Christ guys, which means a lot if you know what I mean; each of us familiar with the right and wrong that had been drilled into us while growing up. He was still active in the church, but I wasn't... except in my head. After eighteen years of going to church three times a week, I'd decided I was no longer interested in denominational religion. My belief in a higher power was intact, and my search for spirituality continued.

I kept calm throughout the interview and felt that it went well. Besides everything Rick and I had in common, I also had a lot of real estate experience in public accounting, which was a plus. During the interview, I tried to focus on his thoughts, not mine, so I wouldn't reveal the trepidation knocking around in my knees. Most important, throughout the interview, I was able to keep a secret I had to myself...

I left the coolness of the office, stepping slowly into the hot day. I knew Rick was watching me through the large window as I slipped into my oven of a car. I loosened my tie as I drove down the service road. I was replaying the conversation I'd just had, trying to sort out how I felt about it, and what Rick thought of me, when I realized I'd missed the on ramp to the highway. I turned around and tried to think about relaxing, but thoughts kept racing through my head. The more I thought about it, the more I anticipated a new anxiety—having to wait for the phone call for a second interview.

CHAPTER 3
Dondi Blue Sky Days

It was a couple of days before I heard back from the Dondi Group. Robbie, Dondi's executive secretary, called and asked if I could meet with Mr. Dixon and Mr. Ramsey on Friday.

"Yes, what time?"

"10:00 a.m." she replied. "Will that work for you?"

"You bet," I said. "See you then. Thanks." The phone call had taken me by surprise. I had already developed a deep sinking feeling that someone else might get the job. My intuition is usually pretty good, and I've found I'm even able to anticipate future events or pick up on hints that I'm being talked about by people at a distance, but if I'm stressed, I pick up misinformation on things still in the making.

This time, I parked at the side of the building, not wanting to be on display again through the looking glass window. In the reception area, just as I was beginning to notice the western art (there was a lot of it), Robbie retrieved me and escorted me to Rick Ramsey's office. He seemed relieved to see me, signaling his readiness to launch the plans with my being part of them, and that gave me a burst of confidence. We talked for a bit, and he asked if I had any more questions.

I had a mental list of questions prepared, starting with who I would report to, who I would answer to, what the future organizational chart would look like, and how long it would take to accomplish the growth. His answers were clear and precise.

One of the interesting aspects of the controller position with Dondi, was that the company was planning significant growth in the near future. The upcoming growth was that Dondi Group would become a parent/holding company, and subsidiaries—individual corporations—were being created for each business purpose, such as Dondi Marketing, Dondi Construction, Dondi Housing, Dondi Builders, Dondi Design, Dondi Commercial Properties, etc. Each company would have its own president responsible for the operation and profit of the subsidiary.

Knowing that he was only going to get one shot at getting it right on who he hired for the controller, Rick confided that he had put himself under a lot of pressure to make sure he chose the right person. Time was certainly of the essence here, and he wanted me to know there was no room for error. Startup companies aren't so easy to manage coming out of the gate, especially when they're about to grow astronomically from scratch.

As we talked, Don Dixon, origin of the Dondi acronym and chairman of Dondi Group, arrived and began settling into his office, just on the other side of Robbie's desk. Seeing a visitor and remembering that Rick had said I would be there for a second interview, Don came into Rick's office and said, "So, who do we have here?"

Dixon was as tall as Rick, maybe even taller. He was tanned and wore a leather vest without a coat, which along with a white, open-button shirt and gold chains gave more emphasis to the western look. (I soon learned that ties were not just unnecessary, they were frowned upon.) Dixon and Rick both wore dress cowboy boots, an organizational style of dress that I would adopt when I could afford it.

Dixon remarked that the three of us had mustaches, so I should fit in well. He didn't stay to visit; he didn't seem the type. Appearing preoccupied with more important things to do, he excused himself by saying, "Carry on, Rickie Wayne," and disappeared across the hall into his office.

The tone of our ensuing conversation changed with Dixon's arrival-departure. As usual, my immediate and automatic reaction was that it must have been something I said. I hadn't said much, but I still felt I'd done something wrong.

***

After getting the job at Dondi, my initial task was to search and find software to load onto an undetermined computer, all within budget of course, and within a short time frame. While figuring all this out, I was to simultaneously begin hiring and training accounting staff that would eventually top out at about 15 to 20 people, including an assistant controller.

My early days were spent searching the market for accounting software that could handle multiple joint ventures, needing detailed cost reporting and financial statements. I had searched for accounting software and computer systems many times before, so it wasn't a dark alley experience for me.

The job came with a bookkeeper, a woman who had transitioned with Dixon and Ramsey from their previous small quarters. She seemed pleasant enough but not very engaging. As her boss over the first couple of weeks, I learned she didn't like being told what to do or how to do it. At that time in my life, personal conflict was not one of my specialties, and I began to realize the bookkeeper arrangement wasn't going to work. After agonizing over it for a few days, I mustered enough courage to explain my difficulty to Rick and asked if she was a sacred cow. He smiled and said, "Do whatever you need to do to get up and running, because we are all going to be very busy, very soon."

Since there were only six of us in the beginning, I felt my secret to be safe. I had recently "graduated" from group therapy sessions with Dr. Brown, but I still needed to continuously work at maintaining a positive opinion of myself, when possible.

My office was located toward the back of the building. Somewhat secluded, I could meditate 15 to 20 minutes in the afternoons by simply shutting my door. I wasn't on medication, but I was definitely missing my therapy sessions.

To get me to take a deeper look within, Dr. Brown often described me as the walking contrast, chipper on the outside, crashing on the inside—how people would never know that a confident looking, almost strutting, 32-year-old young man could close his door, take a seat on the sofa, and completely collapse into an emotional pile.

His steady counseling during my individual and group sessions calmed the fretting boy inside me, the sobbing, hysterical three-year-old who was left behind, who couldn't stop fixating on being a failure. After almost thirty years, I was still blaming myself for having done something wrong.

***

It was an exciting time at Dondi Group. I had begun training my new staff. Rick was finding, interviewing, and making offers to prospective presidents for the various Dondi subsidiaries. The presidents already on board were hiring, and Dixon was somewhere courting investor partners for multiple joint ventures being formed to construct and sell one thousand plus condominiums.

I didn't see much of Dixon, but then again, we operated in different worlds. We both seemed to have uncertain feelings about each other, and this didn't go away as time went by. He was mostly gone, which was okay with me.

As time passed, I learned Rick was an interesting guy, but lonely. One of his pastimes was studying Machiavellian history and tactics. Applying this daily to his team of subsidiary presidents, he anticipated all of them to attempt to rock his ship and toss him overboard and out of his presidential chair. I visited with him most days, having realized he needed someone to talk to. Because of our similar backgrounds, there was no better person for him to confide in than me.

He had sold Bibles in Alabama during his high school summers and taught kids the book of Acts in Sunday school. A Semper Fi Marine, who had married his high school sweetheart before going off to Nam, he was a good guy with great determination; nothing half way, always 100 percent. He liked to say to me, "Beware of controllers bearing gifts." He favored giving people a second chance. And I was one of those people. He gave me a job when I needed it most.

I remember sitting across his large desk observing his bad habit of chain smoking. He had a large, round ashtray teemed with used cigarette filters, lining the glass rim one after another. I enjoyed the visits with him, as they informed me of our progress, new plans, who could be trusted, and who could not. Being the bean counter in the back, I usually had my head down concentrating on meeting the next deadline.

Like most everyone else, I had my good days and my bad. The winds of change seemed to be blowing by me with the world along with it. I was so focused on what I had to do at work that I didn't pay much attention to the news. As a nation, we were still feeling the hangover of the hostage situation in Tehran, and then even worse, from a botched rescue attempt. A sense of failure hung in the air, accompanied by doses of anger and helplessness. Welcome to the club.

The economy was reeling from a 21.5% prime rate, resulting in a gloomy slowdown for the construction industry. The parallel effect was mortgage rates in the 15% range, but of course this was something that didn't cause an appropriate reaction from an unconcerned Dondi Group. Meeting the challenge and pressure from Dixon and Ramsey, we often heard, "We'll sell our way out," from J. Marketing, our guy in charge of sales.

I could hear a lot of laughing from down the hall when he was interviewing with Dixon and Ramsey. The story goes that his shoes looked more like pink pumps than Italian loafers. He still denied wearing any such thing, but it wasn't an issue. He'd soon be wearing dress boots like the rest.

A Kenny Rogers look alike, he often entered the radio sponsored look-alike contests, but never won. My thought was that his being a little on the chubby side cost him any chance of placing in the top three. He was outgoing, very likable, and had the personality not only for the contests, but for his job in which he was primarily responsible for the sales staff at the various condominium projects. We now had six or seven locations in the DFW area, which meant he was herding cats all over the Metroplex.

There was much calamity in the world, there was much calamity in my own personal world. My first wife and I weren't growing closer as time passed, just the opposite. We had survived joint therapy, so we were at least civil toward each other.

It all probably stemmed from my emotional cave in from a bout of heavy depression the year before when I was between jobs. I needed support from her, but never really got much. Although she was well intentioned, she just didn't know how.

She experienced some of the same, having grown up blaming herself for giving her mother polio during pregnancy. Of course, it was impossible for that to happen. Nevertheless, carrying the extra weight of blame for something she didn't do was hard on her. She received little emotional support from her family, which later limited her ability to provide that support to others, including me. She tried, but the well was dry. I filed for divorce, which was finalized in March of 1982 after a heated custody battle. I was awarded custody by the judge: it was a Kramer vs. Kramer like event.

My late afternoons and evenings were filled with sports. My twin sons were athletic. Having played most all of the sports growing up, save soccer, I began coaching their football and baseball teams. I assisted with the basketball team, but I hadn't played much basketball, because I was a wrestler and those two sports were seasonal competitors.

I was beginning to experience successes with the installation of the software and computers; both the people I'd hired and the training told me I was on the right track. The monthly reporting and meetings with our partners were all going well, even the one time the computer blew up and I had to work all night to be ready for the investor meeting the next day.

I remember one time when I was the last to take a seat at the conference table, Rick jokingly quipped, "Dollar waitin' on a dime." I soon learned that it was one of Rick's favorite sayings, and while I understood the humor, I could never find it funny.

It was a reminder that as the controller, I was the lowest paid "executive" in the company. Each of the subsidiary presidents was making $75,000 per year, and your seriously overworked bean counter was making all of $42,000 per year.

***

I was coming up on my one year work anniversary and did not know what to expect. Because I was handling the payroll, Rick knew I was aware of what the others were making for their nine to five work weeks. My work weeks probably averaged 50-55 hours, but I made no mention of it and put my faith in Rickie Wayne, believing that he would reward me for my hard work. I was totally dedicated, coming in extra early to be able to leave in the afternoons during football and baseball seasons, since I coached my boys from the second grade until they went into middle school in Coppell.

I was beginning to develop a decent reputation at Dondi, known as a hardworking, reliable, friendly guy. People were beginning to show some respect for me. I was almost to a point of not considering myself a failure, slowly feeling better about myself and the world about me.

CHAPTER 4
Dondi to Vernon

1981

Dondi Group Inc. (or DGI) created a new holding company, Dondi Financial Corporation (or DFC), which acquired Vernon Savings and Loan in Vernon, Texas. Dixon made Woody Lemons from Vernon its president. At that time, Vernon Savings was an $80 million shop, meaning $80 million in footings, or totals, on its balance sheet. It was in dire straits, losing money to the tune of $10,000 a month, as stated by Woody. It seemed to be well managed, but it couldn't continue down a dead-end road. Because of the imbalance of what the assets were earning versus the cost of deposits to raise money, it was doomed under this old model.

Already targeting larger aspirations, Dixon had arranged a meeting with the Texas Commissioner of Savings and Loans, in Austin. I was asked by Rick to prepare financial statements for DGI. In preparation of the balance sheet, I wrote off some dormant accounts receivable that totaled about $175,000. It was a basic adjustment to an asset that was incorrectly valued. I didn't seek approval for the write off because it was the right thing to do.

***

At one point, Dixon and friends boarded a private jet at Addison Airport and settled in for takeoff. About halfway to Austin, Dixon began reading the financial statements and discovered the write off and its effect on net income. Witnesses tell me that he became enraged. In a tirade, he ripped the pages from the binder and tore them one by one.

Upon Dixon's return, Rick told me that he had to convince Don not to fire me, but to put me in corporate exile instead for me to be repositioned. My job was definitely in jeopardy, my career uncertain.

According to Dixon, I was considered the organization's "untrusted." Yet, they didn't fire me. Rick Ramsey, like me, was a straight arrow. He protected me, referring to it as keeping me out of the box. He was attempting to keep the boat on the straight and narrow and knew that I would be needed to assist.

This was one of my early encounters with the abyss, a place accessible through your heart where deep self-examination is known as soul searching. Had I done the wrong thing? Had I done the right thing? I didn't want forgiveness for doing a right thing. I decided that I would last longer, both mentally and physically, if I stayed out of sight and out of the way. Hello exile.

CHAPTER 5
The Compliance Guy

During 1983-84, as things were so slowly shifting in Dallas from Dondi Group over to Vernon, I stayed busy with compliance as Vernon Savings was under a supervisory agreement imposed by the Federal Home Loan Banking Board (FHLBB). Having these tasks and others, I gradually became an admin guy on the Vernon Savings side of things.

I no longer was responsible for Dondi Group accounting. Rick Ramsey hired someone to become the CFO and run the Dondi Group accounting department. Of course, I was still in exile and Rick continued saving me from Dixon for a better purpose. I was not to be noticed by Dixon. Rick was effectively hiding me.

I appreciated what Rick did for me, and we apparently went back further than I realized. In 1963, when I was around 14 years old, I was in Waxahachie, Texas delivering a letter to my aunt Claudie who managed the local Dairy Queen. While standing outside the order window, I could see through to the back where a teenage guy was working at an astonishing speed. He was back and forth, back and forth flipping burgers, tending fries, and preparing all the other stuff people ordered. It was a hot day, and he was hot and sweaty, but this guy never faltered, didn't miss a step. I was impressed. My aunt finally came to the window, and I left thinking, I was glad I wasn't that guy in the back.

In early 1983, I was talking with Rick's wife, who mentioned that he had worked at the Dairy Queen in Waxahachie. I responded with the fact that my aunt Claudie used to run the place.

She replied, "Yes, that would have been Mrs. McCoy, a real mule driver. She was one tough person to work for." Not long after that conversation, I put two and two together to realize that the guy in the back on that hot day was Rickie Wayne, my boss at Dondi Group. What a small world we live in.

***

Vernon Savings had its own accounting department with its own chief financial officer. It dealt with day to day transactions as they occurred; business as usual. Vernon Savings did not perform any sort of due diligence that I'm aware of, on whether or not the transactions were good sales or good deals, or good loans or bad loans. They would receive the closing statements and documentation to record what came their way and voila, profits resulted.

Still a CPA, I was the officer of Dondi Financial and Vernon Savings, responsible for working with the partner in charge of the audit from Arthur Young, a nationally recognized accounting firm. I discussed reporting theory on various matters, whether recognizable in terms of revenue recognition, income and profits. I did not do any of the nuts and bolts accounting. I did not have any daily accounting responsibilities. Once I was placed in exile, it was the end of day to day accounting for me.

I did not do any type of review on any loan. If I had asked to review a loan (and I didn't have any reason to ask) I most certainly would not have been allowed to do so by Dixon or Woody. They kept a pretty tight rein on their deals, because of what they were doing with them. What they appeared to be doing turned out to be completely different from what they were actually doing.

I spent a good deal of time working on a loan manual and guidelines for the loan guys in Dallas. Of course, they never paid any attention to these materials, only to what Dixon told them to do.

I recall an almost all-day seminar held in Beaver Creek. I was the on-stage presenter. Listening to the new rules, Dixon would groan, and afterward he would often accuse me of pissing on their camp fire.

What I didn't know then, but would find out later, was that the acquisition, development, and construction (ADC) loans were frequently fraudulent. They were often fictitious, put together by Dixon and Woody with certain selected borrowers (deal guys). This may sound simple, but it was created and executed by a couple of master minds. Funds from these loans/deals were used by Dixon for various things like beach houses, airplanes, and art, to name just a few.

I remember a fake dollar bill created by the Dondi Group marketing staff that had Dixon's picture on it with the words "In Don We Trust."

***

In the spring of 1983, a new plan was hatched by Dixon to take the Dondi Group projects and inject them into Dondi Financial, the holding company, via a reverse merger. Vernon Savings and Dondi Financial applied for, and received, approval from the Texas Savings and Loan Commissioner for the reverse merger. Briefly, a reverse merger is basically the acquisition of a company (Dondi Group) by another company (Vernon Savings and Loan), so that the acquiring company gets the benefit of the acquired company's assets and the reorganization of capital.

This became somewhat of a common practice for S&Ls because it was a method of increasing needed capital, which had dwindled during the last few years. Speculators and real estate developers were encouraged to buy savings and loans. They had grand plans of infusions and other methods to increase the capital base. But in this process, the regulators didn't realize they were taking on a boatload of bad assets that on paper looked good. Dixon ordered a massive effort for the reverse merger to occur post-haste.

Just prior to the capital injection merger, there was a supposed buyer for Dondi Group out of Oklahoma. He was a chubby guy who, at a moment's notice, could make his eyes well up with tears, like he was crying. This ploy was to generate whatever sympathy he needed during any negotiations. Dixon had asked Rick Ramsey, who was still president of DGI, for DGI's consolidated financial statements so the proposed buyer could have a better understanding of the purchase price.

While Dixon was meeting with the teary-eyed prospective buyer, a birthday party was in progress downstairs for Rick. I was the chosen one to go upstairs to find Dixon so he could join the party. I poked my head into his office and said, "Come on down. There's a birthday party underway for Ramsey."

What I did not know then was that only a few minutes earlier, Dixon had looked at the financial statements with the prospective buyer and proceeded to throw a fit, a tumultuous tirade of yelling at Ramsey in Ramsey's office. "You're nothing but a bookkeeper. You don't know what you're doing, you're not cut out for a high position." Dixon threw the financial statements against the wall, again yelling at Ramsey so loud that people in the office next door heard it.

What prompted Dixon's explosion was that Ramsey had previously instructed the CFO of DGI to prepare all financial statements according to proper protocols, in accordance with generally accepted accounting principles. Rick had authorized the write offs of a number of items, that were dead assets which had no value.

Neither Rick nor Don attended the birthday party. That was the day when Ramsey's departure was set ... on his birthday.

Rick would learn that his successor would not come from the inside group that he had practiced his Machiavellian tactics on. Instead, someone from the outside toting a bag of better asset opportunities was coming.

Shortly after missing his own birthday party, Ramsey was bought out as president, selling his DFC stock at over a million dollars. He became the only person to ever sell their stock for real money.

CHAPTER 6
A Regular Date

It was September 1983. Dondi accounting staff had arranged a Friday evening happy hour at close-by Shotgun Willie's. Only one week earlier, I'd been having a beer with an old high school friend. I'd told him that I had lost all faith in meeting a woman that I would want to marry. For over a year I had dated a lot, meeting lots of women who I had a lot of fun with, but no one seemed to be the one I was looking for. I had reached the point of giving up because I now concluded she didn't exist. My friend agreed. "Sometimes it works out that way, doesn't it?" he said. I replied that I was tired of looking. "No more expectations," I said.

The Friday evening happy hour event at Shotgun Willie's included both Dondi accounting staff and some people from Texas Instruments. After sizing the place up, I began to mix in with the crowd. Arriving at a booth where three women were sitting, including my friend Karen from Dondi accounting, I stopped to say hello. Karen made the introductions. To one of the ladies I said, "Nice to meet you, Alice," which drew a quick correction.

"My name is not Alice, it is Alex!" I apologized, and then my intuition kicked in and the message came. I heard the words that had been said to me four years ago by a Dallas psychic named Ms. Harris, with whom I'd had a reading. Her answer to my question, "How will I know it's her?" was "You'll know."

Ms. Harris was an elderly woman with white hair, pleasant, but a no nonsense type of person. One day during lunch at the company I'd worked for that had gone bankrupt, a couple of girls were scurrying about preparing for a visit to see Ms. Harris and asked me if I wanted to tag along. "What's a reading?" I asked. "How do you do it?" They explained the basics and I decided to give it a go. Evoking their ladies first privilege, I had to wait until last. I sat in the living room visiting with Mr. Harris, who rocked in his rocking chair watching TV. Finally, it was my turn. I entered the bedroom where Ms. Harris was sitting. As I positioned a chair across from her, she looked at me and said, "You're getting a divorce." I said, "What?" She repeated, "You're gonna get a divorce." I replied, "I don't want a divorce." She countered, "That doesn't matter, you're a-gettin' one anyway." You could have knocked me over with a feather.

She then began to shuffle a regular deck of cards that she used to interpret futures. My future was coming whether I wanted one or not. I asked, "Why am I getting a divorce?" She said, "I don't know, but you will." Still stunned, I asked. "Will I remarry?" She said, "Yes, to a very lovely woman." Pointing to the side of her temple she said, "She'll come to about here on you, her hair will be slightly lighter than yours and she'll weigh almost as much as you. She's schooled, smart and athletic." "When will I meet her?" I asked. She replied, "Not sure, but you'll know when it's her."

Ms. Harris shuffled the cards again and asked me to cut the deck three times. She proceeded by saying, "I see a lot of lawyers, a whole bunch of lawyers." Since I was a CPA, I figured that meant I was going to be professionally successful. She interrupted my wishful moment to say, "It will be difficult for you, but you'll get through it."

As I look back on that moment, I remember being confused, not knowing what to make of it. The more I thought about it, the more confused I got. As much as I analyzed what she said, I couldn't figure it out, so I stopped wondering about it and left it in God's hands. And the FBI's, apparently.

The happy hour crowd was getting pretty noisy, but I still heard the voice in my head saying, "She's the one." I shook my head to the side like there was something in my ear. I took a calm, deep breath to smooth out the excitement, to see if the voice was gone. But I heard it again, "She's the one."

I didn't argue with myself, because one of me always loses. I'd been waiting for this moment for a long time and could hardly believe it was happening. Alex surprised me with her quick wit and easy-going demeanor. She had a slight accent I couldn't place. Later, I learned her father was Scottish and her mother Australian. After a 20-minute visit, I decided to leave, and said, "Nice to meet you" again.

The following week, I returned from a Vernon dove hunt with a couple of Dondi guys in an RV. They had decided to keep the RV to take to Shreveport, to do some gambling over the weekend.

I got the idea in my head that Alex might like to go, so I got her phone number from Karen. I called her and asked if she would like to take a short trip to Shreveport to gamble in the casinos of Louisiana. I told her an RV would be available for the trip.

She said, "No, thanks."

I asked, "Are you sure?"

She said, "Yes, what if I don't like you and end up stuck in a RV?"

I was a little taken aback at the response, but I could see the wisdom in it. I said, "Then I guess I'll have to ask you out on a regular date."

She replied, "Yes, you should do that."

The next day I called for *a regular date*, and we set it for the upcoming Friday. I could hardly wait.

I drove to her apartment and rang the doorbell. She came to the door and motioned me through the small kitchen to the dining room. She stopped and turned around. She was wearing a gorgeous black dress. I had never seen such a beautiful being. At that moment, I felt like I needed an anchor chained to my ankle or I would float away. My heart was pounding; I mean my heart was triple pounding. Standing across from her, I was dumbstruck, not knowing what to say.

Then she did a full pirouette, smiled a big smile and said, "I am so ready to go." And I too was ready to go and already so hooked, having taken the full line and sinker.

I reminded myself to maintain my cool throughout the evening. I drove to Greenville Avenue where the clubs lined both sides of the street. The first place we tried, looking for dinner, was a club called Champagne Johnny's. We went inside and didn't wait long for seating. After a few minutes, I noticed that she was very quiet. I said, "You have become quiet. What's up"?

She said, "I want to leave."

Not asking why, I said, "Okay, we can do that." And we did.

We got into my car and drove across the street to another club for dinner. We had a good time. When we got ready to leave after dinner, I reached into my pocket for my wallet, but it wasn't there. I remembered then I'd left it on my kitchen counter, but it hadn't made the trip due to someone hurrying too much for *a regular date.*

At first, I felt a little panic, but kept it to myself. Then I felt a wave of embarrassment that she had to buy dinner using her daddy's American Express card. Recently graduating as an engineer from Cornell University, she had not established her own credit yet.

After dinner, we made our way down the street to a club on the other side of Greenville Avenue that had the frog statues on the roof. We went inside and proceeded to dance the night away. Around 11:00 p.m. or so, she said, "I don't think I should dance anymore."

"Why?"

"Because I broke the zipper on the back of my dress." What a beautiful looking black dress it was. She illuminated the room every time she walked onto the dance floor. But, given the current circumstance, it was time to go.

On the way home, she told me what had saddened her and caused her to become very quiet at the first restaurant. The guy she had been dating had told her that he wasn't available that evening for a date. He told her he had family matters to attend to. But there he was inside Champagne Johnny's, sitting across the room with another date. This critical sighting by Alex ended that relationship and paved the way for me, for us.

I remembered a movie scene with a teenage boy surprised at finding a Playboy bunny on his bed. She'd been thrown in through his bedroom window via an explosion outside. The kid said, "Thanks, God!" And after what happened at Champagne Johnny's, I too said, "Thanks, God!"

During my first 14 years on this planet, until we moved to Dallas, everyone I knew called me Johnny. I wondered if it was my name that had attracted me to that restaurant or if destiny had left a trail and waited inside.

We left and headed in the direction of her apartment. I was preparing to cruise back by changing some settings on my car's super-duper stereo system. I thought I could impress her with some more music.

But it wasn't long until she was quiet again. I realized that she had fallen asleep. Her head leaned against the head rest, her face angled towards the window. Some regular date, huh?

I arrived at her apartment complex and gently woke her. I got out and hurried around to the passenger door to help her out. We approached the stairs to her second-floor apartment. As she began her ascent, I said good night and started walking towards my car. I could tell from her facial expression that she was a little surprised. I said I had a good time and would call. I did not kiss her, didn't even try. There would be a month of dating and almost daily phone calls before I would ask for a kiss. And then she delivered.

On our second regular date, at another club along Greenville Avenue, with a large fence around a back yard where we sat, I announced to Alex that she was going to have my children. She later claimed that I had freaked her out, but I don't recall seeing it. During the reading session when Ms. Harris told me I was getting a divorce, I asked her if there would be children with my unknown, to be determined wife. The answer was yes!

CHAPTER 7
The Commander

In the summer of 1984, the Commander came to Vernon Savings from being the assistant commissioner for Texas Savings and Loans. He was from Vernon, Texas, although many people that I spoke with didn't recall him as being from Vernon. But he was born there, grew up there, and left there when it was time. He was older than I, clean-cut, a straightforward, no-nonsense sort of person. He served twenty years as an officer with the Department of Public Safety. It seemed to be a pretty good fit for him to come aboard at Vernon Savings.

Not too long after the Commander arrived, he asked me to come to his office and visit with him. He said he was looking for somebody to assist him, to help with administrative type things. He said he'd been around talking to people and was told I was a pretty good guy, that I was smart, that I knew who was who, and what was what around here. Would I consider working directly under him? Yes, I accepted. He provided me his protection, and my punishment in corporate exile officially ended.

Soon, Woody Lemons and the Board of Directors, with Dixon's approval of course, appointed the Commander to be the Chief Operating Officer of Vernon Savings. Eventually, the Commander's job, more than anything, would morph into making sure that Dixon wasn't doing what Dixon was doing.

What the Commander didn't know was that Dixon had been doing what Dixon does for a long time. There were so many ways Dixon had it set up to do what he did, that there was no possible way for the Commander to find out about them all.

That's because the people who were making payments for Dixon by using loan funds did not work for the Commander. They got their orders from Dixon. The Commander didn't really have any control over them or the details of their transactions.

Without the knowledge to make the changes, to stop Dixon and Woody, he was powerless. He ran out of time. The ship sank before he would discover the extent of fraud and the secret plans that kept it under wraps.   He had thought he was going to be employed by a terrific S&L with the best profits in the state of Texas. He'd done his research before signing up with Vernon Savings. Once he was hired on, it wasn't too long before he began to see some of what was going on, but by then he felt it was too late to do anything about it, and hoped that it was the exception, not the rule. He was, I believe, to some extent overwhelmed after he began to realize he was only looking at the tip of the iceberg. How do you change the behavior of the chairman and the president? I think the situation at Vernon Savings was more problematic than he ever thought possible.

The Commander was the G. Gordon Liddy of Vernon Savings in terms of toughness, his outlook on what he should do, what he should not do, and how he should do it. The Commander never really knew the underlying character or health, or lack thereof, of Vernon's loan portfolio until the end, when he told me he was appalled at how bad things were on the bottom of the ship where the god-awful loans were. He felt strongly that he wasn't part of the process of the past, nor the present, and that he wasn't involved with any scheme. He and I developed a close friendship, trusting each other, and I believe he did not intend to commit any crime. Because he lacked the intention, he told me, he committed no crime. "Remember that, John Boy," he'd say to me. He wasn't there during the early, extreme growth years when his integrity and thoroughness were most needed, when the downward spiral Dixon had propelled us into could have been halted.

CHAPTER 8
Politics

During 1983 and 1984, the political climate for savings and loans was at its peak of activity and would remain so for the next few years. Many of the S&Ls were members of the state S&L association, and all members were interested in the politics of how to keep the Feds from interfering with their "ability to make money." The regulators, or Feds, were becoming more aware that there were misdeeds being done in different Texas savings and loans.

There were many political meetings, one of which the Commander asked me to attend as an observer to determine whether or not the political association was serving its purpose. Our guy, who I called Mr. Political, usually attended, but he often seemed to have an exaggerated view of the political association and its individual members; describing how positive and constructive the meetings were. But we didn't see many, if any, results to support his claims.

I attended the meeting in Fort Worth. Jim Wright, Speaker of the House in the United States Congress, was there to orchestrate the show. I don't think I've ever seen a man with eyebrows larger than Jim Wright's. The room was like a large classroom filled with owners and employees of Texas S&Ls. Not in attendance were the regulators, the feds, who were considered the opposition. I took a seat in the back to observe as the meeting was about to begin. I was particularly interested in those behind the podium, those who appeared to be busy updating the agenda and delivering messages. Those in front of it were just visiting with each other, talking about the best way to fight the Feds.

I don't recall there being any motions or political actions determined or decided. What I do recall, throughout the meeting, was a lot of hustle and bustle up around the podium and to the sides of the podium. This hustle and bustle mostly consisted of the podium group of folks asking the rest of us for political donations. Besides that, the other thing I noticed was that most of the participants were not tall, which is a kind way to put it. They were short guys. Each short guy seemed to have a very long cigar that wasn't lit. My view of what was occurring was that the people really running the show were a bunch of short guys with long cigars.

I reported that information to the Commander. He got a kick out of what I saw, or at least out of the way I described it. He was also wary of whether or not the people attending the meeting were really a part of the political aspect or movement for the various S&Ls. The Commander had served as the Assistant Commissioner of Savings and Loans for the State of Texas and in doing so, fielded many requests from S&L owners, employees, and other affiliated persons asking for something. From his experience, I believe he developed a skeptical view of people. He wondered whether they were any good or not, and whether they were doing any good or not. After all, they did seem to spend most of their time hustling each other, and asking the S&Ls to make political contributions.

Dixon had separately been involved in making political contributions. Further, he often instructed Vernon Savings and Dondi Group higher ups to contribute as well. He allowed them to be reimbursed by filing an expense report for the political contributions they made. Now, this of course was against the law. I was sometimes asked to remind staff that Dixon wanted them to make political contributions. I would follow up that statement by saying they'd have to talk to Dixon about how to get reimbursed.

Dixon believed that, given enough money, the politicians in Washington, D.C. would eventually clamp down on the regulators. Jim Wright openly sided with the owners of Savings and Loans, being told and believing that there was no wrongdoing going on at the thrifts. History tells us that this was not true. Jim Wright's loss of the Speaker's seat was proof enough of that.

CHAPTER 9
DRPI

From August 1983 to September 1986, I served in various positions at Vernon Savings and Loan, beginning as a vice president and ending as its chief operating officer. During this time, my duties included establishing internal procedures for lending. I developed the Borrower's Loan Guide, which established Vernon's procedures for making loans and processing loans internally.

In mid-to-late 1984, Vernon was experiencing difficulty with certain assets owned by its subsidiaries, one of them being known as Dondi Residential Properties: DRPI. The DRPI projects included various real estate partnerships, condominium projects, and raw land in Texas, Florida, Louisiana, and California.

Although sales of condominiums had begun to decline in 1983-84, DRPI was able to package the projects in a manner that would boost the capital-equity of Vernon Savings. But they were becoming problem projects, and DRPI would soon be facing audit write-downs on the value of the assets, which would result in losses for DRPI. The losses would then flow up to Vernon Savings, the parent.

It was my understanding that sales of the DRPI projects would be to Don Dixon's *stable of borrowers*, as he called it, for a sales price equal to the cost on DRPI's books. I was responsible for seeing that the DRPI properties were sold on terms that would cause the sales to be in compliance with FAS-66, recognition of gains on sales of real estate. I prepared several memos containing the rules for these sales and circulated them to other members of Vernon Savings staff that were working on the DRPI sales.

Don Dixon's actual scheme, as I later found out, was to arrange phony sales of the DRPI projects to "mustache buyers," to avoid write-downs. Dixon and certain other officers would arrange the "sales" to certain preferred borrowers of Vernon Savings. These "sales" were documented to appear genuine when in fact they were phony.

A group of borrowers did exist at Vernon Savings who had developed a preferred status. These borrowers were hand selected by Dixon to purchase the projects. The borrowers who participated in the DRPI scheme could be eligible for future loans from Vernon Savings. If a customer did not participate in the DRPI scheme, the customer would not be given much consideration for future loans, or for renewal of loans that came due.

After Dixon bought the S&L, Woody became the president of Vernon Savings. It didn't take long for Woody to become busy with Dixon's deals, so Junior from Vernon was appointed the new president and moved to Dallas. Woody became Vernon's Chairman of the Board.

Junior was thrilled to be the president of Vernon Savings. He liked the bright lights, the big cities, the jets and the trips. He just couldn't get enough, it really went to his head. Junior always carried a couple of hundred dollars in his pocket to entertain the ladies he might meet on the road. I liked Junior; he was a likable guy. But Junior always had a drinking problem, always. He drank to get drunk. There was no middle. In fact, a lot of people who worked for Vernon Savings had drinking problems.

DRPI sold the projects under the scheme for the amount that the DRPI and Vernon Savings had invested in the project, as dictated by Dixon. These projects could not be sold on the open market for the price Dixon dictated. Many of the sales of properties were made at a price that exceeded the appraised value of the property.

For those properties sold at a price in excess of the appraised value at the time, additional loans were made on an unsecured basis so that the full "sales price" of the DRPI property could be loaned to the borrower.

The loan documentation called for interest on the DRPI loans to be due semiannually. However, the DRPI borrowers understood that they would not have to actually pay any interest to Vernon Savings on these DRPI loans, and they would be provided with another vehicle such as another loan or another entity from which to make the interest payment. When the interest actually came due, another scheme was concocted that in reality allowed Vernon Savings to fund the interest payments to itself.

Without any regard for the stated rules of compliance or proper recognition of gains on sales, Dixon had secretly structured the DRPI sales.

"Fantasy partnerships" or syndications, which held interest in certain DRPI properties, were created by Vernon Savings and its affiliates. Dixon's scheme was that these "fantasy partnerships" would "sell" their DRPI assets to borrowers in a "repurchase" of the DRPI property. Unsecured loans were intentionally omitted from the loan closing statements so the federal examiners would not notice that the total loans were in excess of appraised values.

CHAPTER 10
The Phantom

I was told that Dixon's deal guys, Dixon's *stable of borrowers*, were all wealthy, with large amounts of cash in the bank and large amounts of equities and so forth. I figured they would have had to be wealthy in order to do these deals. What I found out later was that most of them didn't have anything. They were looking to Dixon to take care of them. While Dixon manipulated them, taking care of himself, no matter what kind of a deal they did, he would give them an indemnification letter, which said that if anything ever happened, he would indemnify them 100%. The promises by Dixon turned out to be worth nothing, absolutely zero. They were worthless.

The Phantom was an engineer who lived in Florida. He was involved in one of the savings and loans there, probably Big Blue in St. Pete, and was introduced to Dixon. He had a lot of energy and a pretty good wit. He was not a big guy, about 5'8" and 140 pounds would be my guess. He was described by the Dallas secretaries as "funny," "sneaky," and "not a sharp dresser."

Dixon hired him to do whatever Dixon wanted him to do. He had no objections to anything. Later, the FBI would describe him as having no conscience whatsoever. The Phantom became Dixon's anointed.

I recall a time, right after my senior year in high school, my friend William and I heard about a party over in the Woodrow

Wilson High School district. A pajama party, as they used to call them in those days, and we were interested in checking it out. William and I had either dated or considered all the girls from our own high school, so we were always looking around for girls that went to other high schools.

When we arrived, there were a lot of people gathered in front of the house. As we were walking across the front yard of the house next door, we were told to leave. We left, waited a minute or so, then said to each other, "Why are we letting these people tell us what to do?"

So, we turned around and headed back to the party. All of a sudden, six or eight guys lined up, forming a wall in front of us about fifteen to twenty yards away. They were large guys, a bunch of football players, who said, "We don't want you here at this party."

We replied, "We're not going to hurt anything or anybody."

They said, "We don't want you here." In so many words, they were saying we don't want you messing with our women! It was like a bull moose standoff. I think a few of them wanted to paw at the ground and blow smoke out their nostrils.

Then this little guy, standing behind the row of big guys, appeared. He was jumping up to see who we were and what was going on, and every time he jumped you could barely see his head between the bigger necks and taller shoulders. When he jumped, he would say, "Go away, go away, we don't want you here." Then he'd jump again to say, "We're going to kick your ass if you come and try to take our women."

One day at the office, there were some people talking about being from Dallas. The Phantom said he was from Dallas and he had gone to high school at Woodrow Wilson. Boom! That's when I connected with his voice. Guess who the jumping jack turned out to be? The Phantom!

The Phantom was the guy at Vernon Savings that you could never find when you needed him. I hung the moniker on him, and everybody else called him that, too. One minute you would see him in his office, and the next minute he would just disappear. He would disappear all day and half the next day. You couldn't find him anywhere.

Later, I learned that his cousin, another outside buyer type that Dixon brought in to try and help save the ship, would meet the Phantom at around 9:30 or 10:00 every morning. They would disappear and both go get drunk. My guess is they could no longer deal with what they were involved in and couldn't find a way to get out.

CHAPTER 11
Christmas 1985

On a windy fall afternoon in 1985, I sat across from Dixon, his spacious antique desk elevated by a four-inch-high stage, for the high-priest-throne effect. Feeling unusually comfortable—I normally shook on the inside when I was around him—I proceeded to tell him that because I had corporately survived longer than any other executive, I was likely to be the one to someday write the book.

I don't recall my visit having a special purpose; the few one-on-one meetings with him over the years usually had a definite purpose, like finding a way to prevent his wife's design company's checking account from getting overdrawn.

I described for him that during the past five years, I had been the corporate piano player. Daily ducking and dodging the bullets that felled many another, my longevity was due to minding my own business and quietly playing on. I had seen many execs come and just as many go. Like the saloon cowboys in an old western, some were out drawn fair and square, and some got it in other ways. Me, I just kept on playing the upright, keeping my head down, staying out of the way, trying not to be noticed, searching for a profile even lower than the one I already had.

I won't forget the way Dixon looked at me when I told him I planned to write a book someday. It was out of character for him to show any unplanned response, but he had quickly flashed a weird-eyed look, best described as a fight or flight combination of "you wouldn't dare" and "you have no idea what's really gone on here."

I was a little nervous from catching this look, but when it quickly vanished I interpreted it to impatiently mean: "Are you finished yet? I have something important to take care of, big deals to do. Get out of here."

***

In December 1985 as Christmas was nearing, there was lots of activity among the execs, including booking profits, booking loans, looking for transactions that made profits and of course increased the pool of the bean plan, which meant bonuses.

I had watched for most of that fall as partnerships were formed to buy the properties, now known as the DRPI deals. The DRPI deals were the condominium projects that were reverse merged two years before.

Dondi Group no longer had the wherewithal to maintain the complexes on a daily cash flow basis. Shoving them up into Vernon meant that they would "always" be paid for. This type of transaction required the approval of the Savings and Loan Commissioner of the State of Texas.

In the fall of 1985, the Dallas effort was to package and sell the DRPI properties to individuals thought to be members of Dixon's *stable of borrowers.*

Raleigh, an ex-college football player from the 1950s and a former partner of Dixon's in the single-family home business known as RalDon, was put in charge of this task. Raleigh was built like a pulling guard, probably the position that he played. As he ambled down the hallway, you would sometimes see his hand and shoulder hitting the wall.

Dixon put Raleigh in charge of getting appraisals for all of the properties. I never met the appraiser, but he appeared to have done an exceptional job—or played an exceptional role—in getting Dixon the values that he wanted.

Originally, these properties were being packaged for sale to various investor-type borrowers, who turned out to be nothing more than mustaches. In viewing all of this from my administrative post, it was my task to see that the gain recognition would be met through compliance with the accounting rules. It never occurred to me that there would not be a real person on the other end of the deal.

There was a lot that had to happen in order to get the deals through compliance standards, not only by me, but by lots of other staff. The last piece of the puzzle was to get the documentation ready for the partnerships that were created for the buyers. Every day we were told, any day now, any day now the documentation is coming from either the attorneys or the loan officers. It's been reviewed and some of the buyer/borrowers are actually signing, etc.

But one evening, a week before Christmas, Woody came into my office, closed the door, and told me that none of the documentation was finished. He blamed Raleigh and his group for that not getting done.

Woody was smart, owl looking, wore glasses and custom dress shirts with button down collars and monograms. He had an insincere look on his face most of the time, almost as though he had something up his sleeve, a look that said he knew something you didn't. He had a sort of perturbed look when having his picture taken, producing a small smirk when the photographer said, "Smile." Not a bad smirk, just his smirk. In spite of his appearance and his looks of insincerity, I actually found him to be kind and polite, not one to take advantage of people. But he was still a deal guy. My view was that Raleigh had probably done everything he could to get it done. Woody explained that he had now involved himself in the matter personally, and that he would see to the completion of the documentation within a period of no more than 30 days. He then asked me to go ahead and make the interest payments on the DRPI loans from another partnership that had already been created with a group in California.

I was reluctant because these matters aren't supposed to be done this way. But I agreed to do what he was asking because he said he was now involved, and I never thought he was untrustworthy. I kept my reluctance to myself, and would go ahead and make the advances to the partnership to pay the interest on the loans, so that they would remain current on the books.

The advance to the partnership was only $1.2 million. I knew that if the documentation did not come together within 30 days as Woody said it was supposed to, I could always reverse the advance in the future. Even though I had reversing the transaction as a potential remedy, it didn't sit very well with me. But I did it because Woody had pressured me. He was a very serious man and always appeared to have a somber expression on his face. At that point, I had no reason not to trust him, and I believed him to be telling the truth.

What I didn't know was that quarterly reports were filed with the Federal Home Loan Bank Board by the people in Vernon. Because I agreed to make the partnership advance to pay the interest, $15 million in loans were classified as current and not delinquent.

The next work day, after Woody's visit to my office, I told Mape, our tax guy, to make the advance to the partnership and ask Vernon to figure out how the advance should be applied to the other unformed partnerships. He and Fir, our audit guy, took it upon themselves to make an attempt at being cunning, by making payments to various Dallas branches using accounts set up by themselves. They thought it would look like the payments were made by the unformed partnerships themselves.

They held the branches open past closing time to get it done "timely"... on New Year's Eve!

I didn't find out about their payments contrivance until the first week of January. I put two and two together on what had happened, called them both into my office and shut the door. They said they were going to tell me, but hadn't got around to it yet. They thought they were extremely shrewd and acted as though they were due some sort of accolade.

I berated them, saying "You guys should not have done that. You should have left it alone as a single payment contribution to the partnership allowing the Vernon people to allocate it as required."

Mape was a CPA who had formerly worked with Arthur Young's tax department. I always thought him to be one of the brightest guys I knew. He had a great sense of humor, and was one of the first I'd heard use the phrase, "That's rich," always with a big belly laugh. He was showing signs of early balding and I often teased him that I was going to get some chalk and draw a line across the upper part of his forehead, so we could tell where his forehead ended and his scalp began.

Fir was the other CPA who worked for me. He fit the mold as the auditor type, but that was good because that's what he did a lot of internally.

Since I was above them in rank, I thought that I would be in a better position than them if some crap came down around us. So, to better fend off the crap, I told them I would be responsible for what they did if it came to that, which of course it did.

In early spring of 1986, when I realized that there was no partnership documentation coming as Woody had promised, I called our audit partner at Arthur Young and asked him to come out for lunch. Mape and Fir joined us, along with the senior auditor from Arthur Young, at a nearby restaurant.

I described to them what had happened and that we were taking care of it by reversing the transaction, which effectively negated the event. Upon hearing what had occurred, their jaws dropped and I thought for a moment they might actually choke on their food.

They took it much more seriously than I had anticipated, probably because I was focusing only on this single transaction. They were looking at it from a much larger view, immediately imagining the possibility of broader ramifications, fearful of what else had been done and what would be next. The FHLBB reports that were filed from Vernon were something that I would someday become well acquainted with.

CHAPTER 12
1986

The gang of four, as I called them, consisting of Woody, the Commander, the Phantom, and Mr. Political, were the top ranking officers of the thrift, who were removed in April of '86 by the Federal Savings and Loan Insurance Corporation (FSLIC). Only a month later, Dixon arranged a meeting for all Dallas employees to attend at the Addison airport hangar where Vernon's jets were kept. After Dixon's speech, in which he announced his permanent departure for California, we learned the other four officers relieved of their duty were not going to return either. Those of us "in the know," or at least we thought that we were, knew that Dixon would not return, because the empire had begun to slowly crumble at his feet. It seems like he made a reference about riding off into the sunset to create some emotional drama, but attention spans were dwindling in the near 100-degree heat. There was no air conditioning in the hangar, just us and the planes.

At that time, we knew that Vernon Savings was the bull's-eye. We knew that it was politically picked on, that it was made a target, a scapegoat, but that Vernon Savings was strong and would endure, according to Dixon. We thought the removal of the top four was rash action. We thought of ourselves as victims. As it turned out, we didn't know the enormous fraud that had been perpetrated by the Chairman and President.

Filling the void, I was appointed by the board of directors in Vernon to be the new chief operating officer. After the hangar meeting, we went to a hotel bar nearby for drinks. There, on steps surrounding an elevated bar area, Mape told me I was his Gunga Din. At first I was confused, but I later remembered the Cary Grant 1930's movie called "Gunga Din," who was the hero for saving many others until he perished in the process. By saying I was his Gunga Din, Mape realized the mistake they had made and was telling me I was his hero for my promise to shield him and Fir, should our world crumble, too. Gunga Din was a Rudyard Kipling hero in an epic poem, and I kept my promise.

Toward the end, on every Friday in Vernon, someone would call to ask, "Are they there yet?" This went on for a few months, as people expected the Feds to come in. One Friday, about eight clone cars pulled up, and fifteen or sixteen agents all dressed the same with matching calculators and briefcases got out and went inside to begin their examination.

During the summer of 1986 as the new COO, I received a lot of phone calls and visits from many borrowers who were promised many things that could not be fulfilled now that Dixon and Woody were gone. I referred to those encounters as rising to the top with an odor. No matter how many times you pressed the handle, it refused to flush. I could not foresee this situation improving in the least, so in September 1986, I resigned from Vernon Savings and the various Dondi entities.

Embracing The Abyss

When I left Vernon Savings, I was under the impression that I was going to have a fine career as a savings and loan consultant, so I established an office with a staff of three people. I had no idea at the time that I had been working for a company that had been involved in fraud, and was responsible for massive losses. It still had not dawned on me what actually happened at Vernon Savings. On the Monday following my resignation, the State of Texas arrived and took charge of Vernon Savings.

Over the next few months, I began hearing a lot of rumors about lawsuits and prosecutions. I was still in touch with the Commander and Woody, as well as with the other people I'd left behind at Vernon Savings who were pondering their futures.

I was angry and frustrated because of the sad condition that the S&L industry was in. I knew the S&L business just as well as anybody and I was as smart as anybody else. After all, look at the success of Vernon Savings. Why shouldn't I be able to go out and help those other sick S&Ls who needed help, such as creating a new loan manual to impress the regulators? But I wasn't able to that because paralysis had set in, causing most thrifts to do nothing.

First of all, you must know what the rules are. You must understand there are rules, that if violated, can result in going to prison. Even after I left Vernon Savings, I had no idea I could go to jail, no idea. Ha, are you kidding me? Me, no way! What for? What did I do?

John Smith

Make sure you understand what can happen. It shows my own naivety, my own unwillingness to challenge my superiors. Hey, they knew the S&L business. They'd been in the S&L business. They were weaned on the S&L business. I believed them. I trusted them. They knew what they were doing. And they never showed me that they were doing anything wrong. Why would I ever suspect they were doing wrong? We're doing so well, how can anything be wrong?

CHAPTER 13
Steve

In the interviews I attended as the representative from Vernon Savings, requested by the FHLBB during the summer of 1986, I heard the law firm Winstead McGuire Sechrest and Minick referred to more than once. Apparently, these attorneys were held in high regard by the officials that questioned me.

So, I made an appointment to meet Bill Sechrest in December '86 in downtown Dallas. I was ushered into Bill's office and he stepped out from behind his desk to greet me. He was a tall guy with a powerful, but not forceful, presence.

I introduced myself, and he asked me to sit down. I sat across the desk from him and began describing the nature of my needs, to see if he felt like he could be of help.

In anticipation of my appointment, he said he had contacted certain individuals at the FHLBB to get a feel for the kind of person he was meeting. He explained the billing structure and the type of legal services he thought might come into play.

After giving this a lot of thought, he suggested that I visit with Steve Brutsché, a friend of his, who was a partner in a smaller law firm in the Cedar Springs area. He described Steve as well-respected by his peers and having versatile skills. He handed me Steve's contact information, then I thanked him and left.

At that point, my only legal need was civil in nature. It concerned my delinquent note to Paris Savings, secured by stock of another S&L, a Woody arrangement that I had been permitted to participate in. Sandia was now crashing down around all those "permitted."

※※※

I called Steve and scheduled an appointment for the coming week. He seemed interested in meeting with me and as I hung up the phone, I was glad that I would finally meet someone who could help me. I sensed that something was beginning, yet ending as well. I couldn't define it, but I had the feeling that whatever it was, had been waiting patiently to occur. Something forged a long time ago was about to begin its own journey.

This particular journey requires for some a preparedness to understand beyond certain scientific approaches, to understand what's known as phenomena. Dictionaries have explained *Deja vu* literally as "already seen" and *Deja vecu* as the feeling of having "already lived through" something. Both of these moments involve a sense of "recollection" with circumstances that may be uncertain or sometimes believed to be impossible.

※※※

A Recollection

There were a number of us in the room, but I don't remember seeing any walls. Rooms are supposed to have walls. It was cloudy, we were cloudy, like looking through smoke through each other. But there was no smoke. Each of the shadow beings moved with a purpose. Plans were being made for lifetimes already assigned with designated outcomes. Some formed soul contracts, our commitment cast as a Divine Agreement. Each of us promised to fulfill the destiny we were assigned and assumed for each other. Parents and siblings were carefully selected for their roles in the creation of long lasting lessons in the upcoming lifetimes.

The Boy, John Smith, was born mid-September in Nashville. His friend and defender, Steve Brutsché, was born less than a week later in Dallas. It would take thirty-eight years for their paths to cross again. It was time for them to begin the undertaking they had vowed to complete in that cloudy, smoky looking expanse without walls.

***

If I could have seen this coming
I would have warned myself, but I knew not.
Had I known in this life what lay ahead
I would have shared such awareness,
Trusting that the understanding
Would be embraced by those still unaware.

Over the years, I have learned that previous lifetimes exist for each of us. Well over 50% of the earth believes in some form of pre-existence. Yes, there really is life again after death. Each new life begins with joy until planned lessons to be learned come into play. The plans you made for yourself to accomplish may not be easy, for they are karmic. They are designed to learn what you did not learn in your previous engagement with spirit and with life. Getting, and then giving your soul a second chance, is a blessing in itself. A higher consciousness awaits for those who ask.

I began to focus on the future. Steve's office was just a few blocks away, and I realized I should've started thinking about the future sooner. His office building was a two-story wooden structure and fit the characteristics of the boutique law firms popping up in this uptown Dallas neighborhood. After coming downstairs to meet me, we headed to his office which had a comfortable feel with lots of pictures of his kids, and the rest could correctly be classified as an organized mess. After all, like me, he was a Virgo; so, things were appropriately in order, just a little messy.

Steve was taller than I and had a slighter build. He had dark hair and dark eyes that were kind. I could tell right away by the way he smiled that he enjoyed life.

We talked a little bit about the issue that had brought me to him, my note at Paris Savings and the stock transfer that would hopefully cure the delinquency.

After discussing the business at hand, I commented on the small replica of a basketball hoop sitting on the corner of his desk. He opened his desk drawer, pulled out some ping-pong like balls, tossed one towards me and said, you go first. Neither of us were any good at it, but both of us were competitive and neither of us liked to lose.

I was lucky enough to meet an attorney who was not only good at his trade, but was good at looking at what life is doing to you, and what you're doing with your life.

In April 1987, four months after Steve and I met, I was sued civilly by the FSLIC for $330 million, which eventually increased to $540 million as they discovered more of Dixon's and Woody's fraud. I was one of seven senior officers at Vernon Savings to be served with the Vernon Savings lawsuit. When you talk about being served with a lawsuit, it's not one of those scenes in the movies or on TV where you see someone avoiding getting served the envelope, trying to tap you on the shoulder or catch you in frustration, trying to run to hide in the bathroom. No!

A constable came to my home in Coppell and asked, "Are you John Smith?"

I said, "Yes, I am."

"I have this for you." He reached to his left, leaned over and dragged a huge box across my front porch to where I was standing. It was packed full of documents: depositions, pleadings, wrongdoings, knowing, fraud, and racketeering.

But I didn't do anything! I just worked there! How could this happen? How could this be happening to me? I worked too hard for this to happen! Why was this happening to me?

After I was served the big box on my front porch, I contacted Steve and told him what I had. He asked me to bring it to him so he could begin reviewing the documents.

Not knowing what I was getting myself into, I bought a new car. My logic was that I soon would no longer be able to get credit for a car loan because of the FSLIC lawsuit. So, I bought a new Jeep Grand Cherokee.

Steve received a notice from the court regarding the civil FSLIC case, asking all defendants and their attorneys to appear in court at 10 a.m. on Thursday morning.

I headed to Steve's office so we could ride together. On the way, I had an altercation. I don't recall doing anything abnormal. I passed a truck. Apparently, the male driver of the truck didn't like getting passed, so he followed me into the parking lot of Steve's office. I parked just to the right of the front steps and stayed in the new SUV to see what this weirdo was going to do.

Out of the truck bounds a tall, skinny, ugly guy with a terrible pockmarked face and a beer bottle in one hand. He headed towards me and my new SUV. He charged me and the car, cussing and swearing, yelling about rich guys that get away with everything. He proceeded to kick in the driver-side door with what looked like a size 10, beat up work boot.

Steve, hearing the commotion, yelled he was calling the police. The combination of Steve's presence and informative language was enough for the guy to jump into his truck and drive away, beer in hand.

As we observed the damage to the door, Steve asked, "Is this your car?"

I said, "Yes."

"When did you buy it?"

I replied, "Oh, a couple of days ago."

"John, you just don't get it, do you? You just don't get it!"

I shared my logic with Steve about it being the last chance I'd have to buy a new car, and it'd be a long time before I'd be able to get credit.

Steve said with pity in his voice, "John, credit is not the issue. After the Feds finish with you, you won't have any money to make the payments on the loan. You need to get ready to be wiped out. Don't you understand that you're going to be wiped out?"

Thus far, his message had not sat very well in my head. I couldn't see it happening to, me because I didn't do anything. I took no money. I committed no fraud. I didn't do anything.

We got in the car and were running a little late due to the pockmark pickup drama. We went to the Earle Cabell building downtown and rode the elevator to the eighth or ninth floor, to find an empty court room. No one was there, only us.

Steve went to the clerk's office in the back to find out what was going on. The hearing had been postponed because the judge didn't think it was a good idea to have all those defendants in the same room at the same time with all their lawyers. I'm guessing Steve had not been in the loop long enough to receive my notices.

I felt silly, thinking on the way over there that I would be identified and relinquished from any further obligation. They were supposed to figure out that I didn't belong in the lawsuit. I was stricken with a total lack of vision about what was going to happen.

We drove back to Steve's office and made plans for me to meet with him, to begin counseling on the new real world: my part in Vernon Savings. The last thing he said to me, as he closed the door was, "Take this car back."

The next day I took the car to the dealership and parked outside the sales office. I found the guy who sold me the car. I told him I couldn't keep the car and was returning it. He was irate. He got close enough to the driver side door and saw the kicked in damage. He then shifted from irate to berserk. He was yelling at the top of his lungs. "You can't do this, you have a contract! You can't do this! Who caused this damage?"

I replied some ugly guy kicked in the door.

The salesman said, "That doesn't matter, you can't bring this car back."

"I don't have any choice. I've just been sued by the FSLIC for $350 million. My attorney said to bring it back. Here it is. I'm sorry."

I developed something comforting to get me through this time, and when I look back I call it my net theory. The net theory goes like this: when going through the fish caught by the net, the Feds will study their catch. Sometimes they catch fish that don't belong in the net, like a Smith fish. I'm one of those fish; I don't belong here. Pretty soon, they're going to let me go. I'm going to get to swim free. I'll leave and not look back because they're going to leave me alone. I didn't do anything. I only worked there.

One thing that I learned from Steve is that lawyers have a grapevine that we civilians don't. They know when things are happening before we do. Because it wasn't long after the FSLIC suit was filed that he began to hear noise from other lawyers that criminal charges against the seven defendants, including me, at Vernon Savings were on their way.

The regulators had moved quickly to organize the Justice Department for an invasion. The FBI had formed and staffed a number of task forces, one of which was in Dallas. The law suit filed by the FSLIC was soon followed by FBI criminal investigations. They came to town looking for blood, guts, and headlines.

An attorney friend of mine formed this view of the FBI guys when he would sit in on meetings, when defendants were being questioned, trying to determine what they were looking at and where they were going. His conclusion was that their attitude was, we don't care who you are or who you were, whether you were the president, the bills clerk or the lawyer representing any of them because all of you are cut out of the same cloth. You're a crook, your lawyer is a crook, your clerks are crooks. We'll just round everybody up and throw them into a pen and let the Justice Department sort it out about who's guilty and who's not.

Steve continued working with me because it didn't matter what I did or didn't do. His purpose was to get me to focus on the large amount of pretense that existed at Vernon Savings followed by colossal denial: mine.

Steve and I had some terrific yelling sessions. Steve had to do that to get me to listen to him. I sometimes just would not listen and only argued in return that I didn't do anything. This almost drove him nuts.

Steve asked me about certain documents he was given by the FBI. He had a copy of the minutes of an executive committee meeting showing me in attendance. I informed him that there were never any executive committee meetings. We soon learned that Dixon and Woody had created fake documents like this. In due time, we would also learn that the minutes of the board meetings in Vernon were also "revised" extensively by Woody and Junior for acquisitions, loan amounts, and delinquent loans.

Up to this point, I don't think Steve was 100% convinced that I was telling him the truth, all the truth. However, he connected with some of the other defendants' attorneys and the FBI, and confirmed what I was telling him.

After all, I handled liquidity as my responsibility during the last year, so in fact I was keeping the pirate ship afloat. What I began to realize from Steve beating on me was that he should have been a nun, and I don't mean the Mother Theresa kind—I mean the nasty school teacher nuns. For instance, if we were sitting at a table talking about what I did and didn't do and I would say, but I didn't do anything, that's when he would pick up the nearest thing to him and hit me with it just to get my attention. He had to beat me up to get me to realize that it wasn't a matter of if I'm going to prison. It was almost a certainty. I was already on my way. No two ways about it, I was already on my way. I just didn't know it, couldn't see it. I didn't do anything. But whether I did or did not, it didn't matter.

I had a lot of questions that I didn't have answers to. I didn't want this, but I couldn't get away from it. I couldn't get rid of it. I didn't want it, but I couldn't give it back. I had to deal with it.

***

My intuition must have been working well. In mid-March, one month before I received the large box, I started seeing Dr. Brown again. I had resumed finding infinite ways to mentally beat myself up, digging up the old, low self-esteem to wallow in. If I could only pile on more and more, I could run through the brick wall and this time, would most certainly deserve to be rescued. But I could not show this side of me to anyone other than Dr. Brown. Allowing others to know about my aching on the inside was a no-no.

It's possible, I suppose, that a tendency towards depression could be genetic and it could also be a result of monkey-see-monkey-do. When I was five or six years old, living in Nashville, Tennessee, I discovered my Daddy sitting on the floor in the living room with his back to the sofa. He was crying. "Daddy, why are you crying?"

He said, "I don't know Johnny."

Because he was crying, I felt like crying, too. I asked my Mama, who was the caretaker, "Why is Daddy crying?"

She said, "Because he's sad."

"Why is he sad?"

"I'm not sure, Johnny. It's a long story."

My younger sister and I had been told not to cry in front of Daddy or he would start crying, too.

Later, I didn't see Daddy around the house and wondered why. I asked Mama, and she said he was at the doctor's. That night we went to visit Daddy at the doctor's.

It was a wooden, one-story building with lots of cars out front. Inside there were rows of beds like you would find in an army barracks, except there were no beds on top of the bottom for a double, only bottom beds. Each bed was occupied by a male person. Mama told my sister and me that the women had their own barracks down the block.

Daddy didn't say much, he smiled a little, but seemed embarrassed that we were there. Knowing what I know now, I would have wondered if the rest of the men with bunks in the building were dealing with PTSD from the Korean War or WWII. Daddy had flat feet, so he was declared 4F, which meant he got a pass on serving in the wars.

Shortly after his stay in the barracks, we moved to Oklahoma City. Soon he would spend a year in the state mental hospital in Norman, Oklahoma.

Years later, I learned what caused Daddy to be so sad: he was suffering from depression. When growing up, he was the youngest of eight children and at age seven, he had continued to sleep with his Mother, Mammy. Then came child number nine, my uncle Roland. Daddy couldn't sleep in Mammy's bed any more. Simply put, he was replaced by another, his brother. My Daddy never got over it. He carried that loss all the way to his grave.

CHAPTER 14
Crossing the Rubicon

Vernon Savings had been under supervisory agreement since the fall of 1984. The FSLIC and FHLBB had placed a cease-and-desist order on the thrift. The cease-and-desist order set limitations on what Vernon Savings could and could not do, such as how fast they could grow over various periods of time. Vernon Savings had grown annually from $80 million in year one to $150 million in year two, then to $330 million, then $800 million, and finally to $1.2 billion by year five. This was phenomenal growth, almost incomprehensible. It was incomprehensible for the people in Vernon, Texas trying to keep up with the loan documentation and accounting. Those were the people who were most overwhelmed by it all.

I see now that their being overwhelmed helped to contribute to a lack of understanding, a lack of information about what was really going on inside the thrift. Vernon Savings was flying 990 miles an hour. There was no chance to stop and look to see where we were going. All we knew was we had to turn that next corner, turn hard and fast.

***

When I pleaded guilty in February of 1988, there was a big announcement by the FBI task force parading three individuals with felony guilty pleas. I was one of the three making the headline news on TV, radio, and in the newspapers.

On the evening of the announcement, I was at home, alone, watching the six o'clock news. The lead story was a major broadcast by the Justice Department, with the message that they were cleaning up the S&L mess, and that they were just getting started.

The news release caught me off guard. No one announced, "Look out, you're going to be on TV." I guess I thought it would be revealed with fairy dust. I sat down to ponder what I'd just seen. Then, the phone rang.

It was my Aunt Joy. "We saw you on TV, Johnny. We want you to know that we still love you."

I choked back a thousand words, muttered, "Thanks for calling," then collapsed, first to my knees and then to the floor.

***

After much wailing and gnashing of teeth, Steve convinced me that I needed to cooperate with the FBI if I wanted to avoid prison. He put it in his own words: you have to cross the Rubicon. As the admin compliance guy, I knew a little bit about most everything, but not a whole lot about one thing. This made me more valuable to the FBI than the other defendants. There was a frantic race going on among the various defendants, each wanting to be selected by the Justice Department as the person to cooperate and maybe get a better offer, and possibly a deal.

"Crossing the Rubicon" comes from when Julius Caesar crossed the Rubicon River with his army in 49BC, accelerating the Roman Civil War that eventually led to his becoming dictator for life of the Roman Empire. There was no going back.

As the FBI task force cleaned house and began their prosecutions, we were forced to choose sides. I crossed the Rubicon, sadly landing against the Commander. I've not talked with him since. My loss. I was accepted and became a member of the other camp, the FBI task force in Dallas-Fort Worth.

And that's when I began searching, researching, and testifying. Day after day, week after week, I would sit in a room full of boxes, each box containing multiple loan folders and files. The more I reviewed, the more I thought, "These don't make sense, these deals don't make any sense. Why would anybody be buying real estate in this economy?"

The reason that the documents didn't make sense was because they were full of fraud. The sales were phony. The purpose of these alleged sales and the loans were to fund the purchase of certain assets from DRPI, so that potentially troublesome assets could be removed from DRPI's books. The profits generated by DRPI through these asset sales would then be reflected on the books of Vernon Savings.

What began to make sense was the pattern of how they would pack the back end of a new loan with provisions to make payments for the jets and the yachts and beach houses in California, or make payments to a borrower who had done himself good by doing a favor for Vernon Savings. This is how Dixon did business to pay for his lifestyle, and did he ever have some lifestyle.

The more I researched and testified, the better I felt about the decision I'd made with Steve's guidance. I understood that I was making a contribution, to what the task force was trying to achieve. It also boded well for me in determining what my sentence would be. Of course, that would be decided and given to me by Judge Maloney.

CHAPTER 15
The Emperor

One of the first things that Steve Brutsché did, was get me to focus on pretense and denial. When he began to get through to me, he told me the Hans Christian Anderson fairy tale of "The Emperor's New Clothes." I didn't understand how the story related at first, so Steve explained it to me and reminded me of it often.

Analogy? The king was Vernon Savings. The weavers were Dixon and Woody, the loan officers and manipulators of Vernon Savings. The ministers serving the king?

I was a minister.

When I finally let go of the pretense, I came to grips with what had happened, with the realization that I had been involved indirectly. But I still, nevertheless, had been involved.

In visiting the abyss, I realized that I wasn't just dotting I's and crossing T's. I was keeping the Vernon Savings tar baby boat afloat by managing the liquidity, an integral part of the overall operation. Even though I didn't have my hand directly on the tar baby, I was keeping afloat the boat. Liquidity was instrumental in providing the wherewithal for Dixon and Woody to do what they did. This is the part that I needed to come to the realization of, for myself and for Steve.

In the coming months, I realized daily that it had all been done with mirrors. One flashing, reflecting on the other.

I realized that the going concern of Vernon Savings was put together and worked, as long as there was a smokescreen of paper profits, of customer funds to fund it.

I had been misled; I had been deceived. My view of the past became much clearer as I began to cooperate; cooperate, yes. My choice of what to do with the lawsuit and the criminal charge hit me. I thought for a long period of time that I was going to be able to sit at the end of a long table, disassociate myself from the others who had made the loans, who had made the promises, and be able to look them dead in the eye and say, "I didn't do anything. That's why I'm trying to sit down here at the end of a long table by myself and know what those people were. I was the bean counter. I was in the back, kept in a dark room."

It was then I realized there was a massive freight train called the United States government coming straight at Vernon Savings, and the people that had worked there. I realized at that time that I needed to crawl over to the side of the tracks so I wouldn't get run over.

Within a few months, I was wiped out financially just paying the lawyers. As I began to cooperate with the attorneys of FSLIC, the Justice Department and agents for the FBI, I began to share my story.

I had a story that no other defendant could tell them, because I had been at Dondi and Vernon longer than anybody. I didn't realize until then that it was going to help me someday.

Embracing The Abyss

I was surprised that I had survived corporately longer than anyone else. I'd seen the cowboys come and the cowboys go. Some of them got gunned down from behind and some straight on. In the saloon, I was the piano player. Minding my own business, staying busy, I just kept playing the piano, keeping my head down. And when the bullets came, I ducked, trying to keep a lower profile than I already had.

My story also came with some credibility, because I was not one who ran socially with the group. I did not run with the pack nor play with the prostitutes. It was one of the ways that I was exceptional. It was one of the reasons I became credible as a witness for the government.

As I cooperated and researched, they made available to me a number of my records, my old files, and other boxes full of documentation. They pulled the ones they wanted me to look at. Do you remember? Do I recall? I've got a great memory, too. What I began to see was more and more about things that didn't make sense to me at the time.

Reviewing the growth regulations and knowing Vernon Savings was about to come under a cease-and-desist order, why were they buying real estate? What I hadn't realized at the time, was that one of those many promised favors was finally being paid off. Somebody along the way who had helped out Dondi-Vernon, was being repaid.

I ran across head-scratching transactions that I would look at and think, why did they do this? I see it now. It made no economic sense at the time. It's that simple.

I also recognized myself during that time. I remember the large number of times I'd glide past on the signing off on any loans. I'm glad I didn't sign anything.

One of the nicknames that had been given to me by the loan officers was "Asbestos." They knew that I would not sign anything unless I had 100% of the documentation and appropriate approval. So, I'm pretty sure I never signed anything for approval that wasn't legitimate.

My responsibilities were liquidity, keeping up with the regulations, business plans, and compliance. It was a full-time job.

I recalled a hunting trip to Kansas, mostly for Vernon's loan executives. After the day's hunt, a group of 10-12 executives were in a bar called something like the Sin Bin in Garden City, which was across the Oklahoma panhandle. One of the local girls dancing with a loan officer had asked what he did for a living. He said, "I lend money." She said, "What do you do if they don't pay it back?" He replied, "Lend them more money!"

Looking back, I know that should have triggered some alarm inside me, but it didn't. By that time, I had acquired all the other operational functions, but still the loans were kept separate. The loans were kept under wing in close guidance by Dixon and Woody, the manipulators, the loan officers catering to them. I know that when I look back, I can see myself ignoring it by looking the other way. It was convenient to do so as I was not involved. After all, how could there be anything wrong? We were so successful.

CHAPTER 16
Criminal Code

In March 1988, I pleaded guilty to one felony count based upon a two part proffer containing an offense and an offer.

THE OFFENSE

On or about December 31, 1985, at the direction of a Vernon senior officer, John Smith arranged for Vernon's subsidiary, Dondi Group, to pay on behalf of the delinquent DRPI borrowers $2,061,000 in interest due on the delinquent DRPI loans, thereby making the loans current as of December 31, 1985. The Vernon senior officer directed Smith to make the $2,061,000 interest payment from funds designated as a Dondi Group investment in Dondi Group's subsidiary, Dondi Properties. In fact the payment, at that time, was not an investment but an additional loan to the DRPI borrowers. By using in effect Vernon's own funds to make the DRPI borrowers current, Smith, although not the officer responsible for the preparation of Vernon's quarterly report to the bank board for the quarter ending December 31, 1985, nonetheless caused the report to be false.

John Smith

THE OFFER

The following is the complete agreement between the Department of Justice and John Smith in which Mr. Smith agrees to enter a plea of guilty to a federal criminal violation and to cooperate with law enforcement personnel in the Northern District of Texas federal grand jury investigation and any trials involving Vernon Savings and Loan and other institutions.

Mr. Smith will waive indictment and plead guilty to an information charging him with a violation of 18 U.S.C. 1001. The information will charge Mr. Smith with a false statement, not under oath, in connection with Vernon's monthly or quarterly report to the Federal Home Loan Bank Board for the period ending December 31, 1985.

Mr. Smith will cooperate with the Department of Justice and agents of the Federal Bureau of Investigation and the Internal Revenue Service in criminal investigations and criminal trials concerning his employment at Vernon. Specifically, Mr. Smith will make himself available for interviews, grand jury testimony, and possible hearings and trials. Mr. Smith will also cooperate with agents of the Federal Home Loan Bank Board and the Federal Savings and Loan Insurance Corporation including attorneys representing said agencies. Also known as the requirement to cooperate with the Bank Board and the FSLIC. The Department of Justice will make known to the court at the time of sentencing the extent of Mr. Smith's cooperation.

After the above plea of guilty, my cooperation with the Department of Justice over the next seven months was critical in the determination of my sentence. Steve and I understood the importance of this crucial period of time, and there were a number of things that we began to work on. My part was to give the Justice Department everything I could and then some. My cooperation with personnel from all federal agencies requesting interviews and information sessions would be of great significance.

Steve was a great communicator and proved himself to be so time and time again. His skillfulness at keeping all those involved aware and up to date was amazing. In analyzing the mission and mission response, he quickly identified the serious impact of the criminal code, its scoring and sentencing guidelines. Steve's ability to change gears from civil to criminal was a saving grace. Quietly working in the background, without disturbing me about what he was facing, allowed me to confidently pursue and perform my roles. We both had specific goals and a limited amount of time before my sentence would be rendered. Mine was the job of trying to stay out of prison. His was keeping me out of prison.

The month following my guilty plea, Steve began to work in earnest with the U.S. Probation Office, as they would be the ones to score and recommend sentences according to the guidelines. He was surprised at the misconstrued view of my criminal offense held by my pre-trial probation officer.

His first letter to her was in March. He strenuously argued that the pre-sentence report did not adequately or accurately reflect the underlying offense. I was charged with a reporting violation, not with the improper disbursement of Vernon Savings funds, and did not cause any direct loss of any funds.

In April, Steve sent a request to the probation office via my probation officer, that my sentence be re-categorized to a lesser one based on the prosecution's own statements as to what had happened, with regards to the loan payments made on the DRPI properties.

As late as August 1988, only six weeks before my day of sentencing, my pre-trial probation officer still thought she needed to grade my offense under Chapter 3 ("Theft and Fraud Offenses"), as a Category Six offense. After receiving notice of this, Steve sent the Justice Department prosecuting attorneys a request for assistance asking for their confirmation that they had no problem with the lesser offense categorization.

Steve had both hands full as he dealt with the difficulty of the federal criminal code, and the mistakes being made by my pre-trial probation officer. How could they continue getting it wrong? Did they always choose the worst interpretations for everyone or was it just me?

Don't answer the last one. If it's going to go wrong, it's me. If it's always screwed up, it's mine. But that's the way it's always been. I was always dealt the most difficult, never the easiest. I surmised it must be preparation for the future, more training for the next unknown task waiting around a karmic corner.

CHAPTER 17
One for the Gipper

It was the summer of 1988 when senior FBI Agent Dale Hogue called and asked me to meet with him and FBI Agent Kirt Hodges. Driving to the FBI office, located in the west end of Dallas, I began to wonder why he had asked me if I knew a guy named Gipp. Arriving in the waiting area, I checked in with the person behind the glass window and sat down. I tried to focus on what the discussion might be, about the Gipper.

Kirt came into the waiting area, asked how I was doing, and said, "Let's go this way." Of the many times I had been in this FBI building, not once had I been taken to a meeting location by the same route. It was always different, through the maze of doors, hallways, and elevators.

We entered a room where Dale was waiting, and we sat down around a small conference table. Dale began by saying, "We've been offered Gipp's testimony in Woody's upcoming trial, and we've been told that Gipp knows you. What can you tell us about Gipp? Do you know him?"

"Yes," I replied, "I know Gipp from high school in Oklahoma City. He was a senior, when I was a freshman. We were on the wrestling team."

Dale opened by saying, "We want your opinion of Gipp. We need to know if we can trust him."

I paused for a bit. "Is he a good guy or a bad guy you mean?" I asked, knowing there wouldn't be an answer to my question. Even though I had worked closely with them both for over a year, my innocent inquiry only brought blank stares. Sensing the seriousness of the matter, my mind raced with thoughts of the past. I swallowed big and took a deep breath. "Let me tell you a story. I think you'll be able to decide for yourselves."

I literally began with "Once upon a time," which brought a slight smile from each of them. Finally feeling a little more at ease about the matter at hand, I continued.

Gipp was the big man on campus at Northwest Classen High School. During the 1962-63 school year, I remember a large crowd gathering in the parking lot alongside May Ave, across from Phipps Appliances and the Sugar Shack. As I worked my way up close to the source of the oohs and aahs, I was surprised to see a brand new Chevy Impala. Wow, what a car! Before I could say "Whose is it?" the name Gipp came rippling through the crowd. But the Gipper was nowhere to be found.

I didn't know much about Gipp then, except for his huge BMOC reputation, and that he was named an all-state quarterback. As a freshman wrestler, I worked out with the others, including most of the upper classmen, in the wrestling room at the end of a long hall, next to the gym. Gipp would qualify for the final rounds at the state wrestling championship that year. Watching the icon practice with Coach Marcotte, who was the only person who could handle him, was a treat.

As the season progressed, we freshmen began to hear rumors about the hazing which was coming from the older guys. Then, we learned that they had already struck the day before by ambushing and trapping a couple of freshmen, including Ralph, who was a big guy. Stripping him, spraying analgesic balm, and applying powder to his crotch area, Ralph's privates were stinging for at least a week. He's still pissed!

Of course, this was a dire warning, and the more I thought about it, the more I was determined not to let it happen to me. The few of us who had not been hazed were constantly on guard, and frankly, quite scared about it all. Soon, the day came when at the end of practice, we were heading down the stairs to the wrestler's locker room located below the wrestling room.

Suddenly, from behind we heard, "Come on, we've got them now!"

My fellow freshmen and I immediately realized that we were hopelessly trapped, with no other way out. We ran down the few remaining stairs and sought refuge in the cage, which sat to the right in the middle of the room, closing the gate behind us. The cage was a floor-to-ceiling metal structure made out of chain link fencing, that was used for odd stuff like hanging sweaty wrestling gear.

We barricaded ourselves against the gate, found some metal coat hangers, and wrapped them around the gate handle and side structure to secure the cage. Three of us were trapped inside the cage, scared shitless, and as the gang of upper classmen grew, we knew a battle was brewing.

A few of the upperclass vigilantes found some metal piping and began to beat against the gate where the coat hangers were wrapped. They were mad, I mean really mad, that we were not cooperating in receiving our freshman initiation. Their yelling, threatening us with everything they could think of, was so loud and angry that it alerted the situation to those who were still upstairs in the wrestling room, where Coach Marcotte would often keep Gipp after practice for more work.

Now way out of control, the uppers had crazed, wild eyed looks. When the fanatics were about to explode with anger, becoming physical and dangerous, Gipp appeared. When they saw him they yelled, "Help us get these bastards out of the cage!"

In a calm voice, Gipp asked, "Why?"

One of the juniors yelled back, "We were going to haze them, but now they've made it worse, so we're going to beat the crap out of 'em."

Stepping towards them with authority, Gipp continued in a calm voice. "Back away. There's not going to be any more hazing, no more. It's time we put an end to this. It's a bad tradition."

The fanatics wanted to argue with him, but they sounded more like wimpy whiners. Their respect for him allowed the Gipper to prevail, and poof! We were saved.

We waited a good 20 minutes after all had cleared the room and gone home before we felt safe enough to come out of the cage.

My story finished, I looked at Dale and Kirt and said, "So, if you're asking me if I would trust Gipp, my answer is completely, and I believe you can, too."

Having a smoking gun now, the government made Gipp a key witness.

Funny, how things that go around, come around. Karma, they call it. Twenty-five years after the rescue from the rage at the cage, I was given an opportunity to repay a karmic debt, a favor to help the Gipper as he had helped me.

CHAPTER 18
Cruella Visits

A pre-trial probation officer for the federal court in Dallas, made arrangements with Alex to visit with her at our home in Coppell. It was an early afternoon meeting on a sunny day by the pool overlooking our backyard.

The officer was a tall woman with long, black hair. She was smug and seemed pleasantly pleased that someone was going to suffer, that someone better off than her was going to become unhappy. As she and Alex sat in chairs on the pool deck, her first question was, "Are you ready for when your husband goes to prison? Because he is going to prison."

Upon hearing these cruel words, Alex shut down. "How do you know that?"

After the probation officer dropped her bomb, she seemed very pleased with herself. She wasn't rude, but she came from a position of power. She wanted to hurt Alex, to see her cry, and she did. It was a serious attempt to take Alex down a notch or ten!

Alex does not recall anything after that. It was a short meeting, not even 30 minutes long.

I arrived an hour or so later to find Alex distraught. Alex's question was why would she want to frighten me? The ground seemed like it was sinking beneath both of us.

Reaching for words, I said to Alex, "It's not going to happen like that. I'm not going to prison." My statement surprised me because it came from a part of me that I usually keep to myself. From the beginning of the problems that Vernon Savings brought, I promised myself that I would not bring it home. With the relentless pressure I experienced every day about jail or no jail, I chose not to talk about any of it with Alex or my sons. I knew that I didn't have an answer for this pending predicament, so I kept it pretty much to myself and prayed a lot.

I explained to Alex that probation officers make a calculation according to the federal criminal code. They score crimes on a point basis, using the criminal code that probation officers and other agents use to determine sentencing guidelines.

When I told Steve about the probation officer's visit and intentionally upsetting Alex, he was livid.

Steve had already discovered a number of mistakes in the pre-trial probation officer's facts regarding my case. However, he set the record straight by providing her the truth on multiple occasions. Her calculations of my doing time dropped more than once based on the information that Steve provided.

For instance, she had me taking dollar amounts and/or receiving dollar amounts, which was simply not true. Her analysis of my case was definitely skewed toward the worst she could conjure.

After Alex's meeting with the probation officer, I was even more resolved not to discuss much about anything regarding

Vernon Savings, the pleading, or the future sentencing while I was at home. I felt that this decision would better maintain both our sanities and allow us to live as ordinary people raising two children.

Waking every morning, I would gaze up at the bedroom ceiling, wondering if I was in prison yet. This was always my first thought and every morning, I had to get that thought out of my head to accomplish the daunting tasks that lay before me.

There were a few occasions when I explained certain things to Alex or answered her questions, but on the whole, we lived our lives as we thought we should, not worrying about the unknown.

I knew deep inside that I had a special purpose in this life, even if it was a small one, and I believed that God was seeing me through to get there. I knew I was not dealing with this on my own, and that I was pulling in strength and guidance from the heavens. I was thankful every day, for every day.

CHAPTER 19
Sentenced

On October 12, 1988, the day before my sentencing by Judge Maloney, Steve wrote and delivered a very moving and convincing letter to the judge, asking for probation instead of prison time for me. As usual, Steve was all over it again, in winning form.

He based his request on my character and history of community service, the low level of my offense, my loyalty to my superiors at Vernon Savings, how I had been misled by them, how I had voluntarily reversed the transaction when I learned of the true facts, and how I had no personal gain from my actions. My conduct, compared to my fellow defendants, was considerably less egregious, and I had assisted the Justice Department and the FSLIC to a great extent. According to government agents, my assistance saved the government literally thousands of hours of investigation and attorney time, and millions of dollars. During that assistance, I never took the Fifth, and I continued to work with them even though their civil suit against me wasn't settled until just a month before.

As part of the settlement, I gave the FSLIC a lien against substantially all equity in my homestead, even though my homestead is exempt from execution and was acquired well prior to my association with Vernon Savings. I gave the FSLIC all I possessed and more than the law would require.

Steve provided the court with letters from people who had known me my whole life. They detailed my academics, my decorated combat service in Vietnam, my volunteer work at the Children's Hospital of Dallas, and community service through the Rotary Club. This included coaching sports, school and other civic activities in the city of Coppell, and most recently, working with disabled children at Scottish Rites Hospital. He spoke about my work on projects related to rehabilitation of low income housing in Fair Park/South Dallas, as well as my lectures to college accounting students on "Professional Responsibilities and Ethics."

Steve concluded his letter by saying, "Mr. Smith's extensive past and anticipated cooperation is but one of four separate and independent justifications for a probated sentence. His past life, character, reputation and community service, and principles of proportionality and sentencing also support a probated sentence."

After my sentencing, I wanted to reiterate the journey of how difficult it was and warn people by telling them how not to do what I did. How can I help you avoid this? Whether you're an employee of a public accounting firm or the employee of a client, how do you avoid this?

The first step is awareness. Because awareness is necessary for consciousness and prevention. It reminds me of the song by the rock group *Yes*. The same words repeat over and over and over: "If it can happen to me, it can happen to you. If it can happen to me, it can happen to you."

I hope to leave others with something lasting they can use, to put in their pocket and take with them into the future. Like inner peace.

CHAPTER 20
As You Wish

On a sunny day after receiving probation from Judge Maloney, I drove my motorcycle, which I rarely rode, over to see Steve at his house. We had become very good friends from all that we had gone through with the Vernon Savings nightmare. He had bought a two-story house to increase his opportunities of having custody of his kids, whom he adored. I think there were five of them, well-mannered and happy as I recall. When I got off my bike and headed toward the door to the house through the garage, I noticed a ping-pong table.

Once upon a time, I won the Northwest Classen high school ping-pong championship as a freshman, by beating a popular junior shooting guard on the basketball team. It was a tough match and he was good. All of the juniors and seniors rooting for my opponent packed the room. I recall only a few freshmen being there, one of whom was my childhood friend Frosty. The upper classmen made a lot of positive noise for my adversary, and even more negative noise for me. I recall a lot of threats and trash talk about how I couldn't win no matter what.

Hearing all the derogatory vocals thrown at me during the match, I had moments on the edge of freaking out.

During short breaks, Frosty said to me, "You can do this, Johnny. You can do it. Keep playing the "D," don't get suckered into trying to slam the ball. Just concentrate on getting whatever he tries back over the net. You can beat him!"

And I did. All the upper classmen were in complete and total shock, including my rival, who left quickly.

Frosty slapped me on the back so many times it stung.

After hanging out with Steve for an hour or so, which included a lesson on how his cat was training to use a regular toilet instead of a litter box, it was time for me to go.

He accompanied me through the door into the garage. As we passed the ping-pong table, he queried, "Do you play?"

"Sure, I've got time for a game."

We picked up the paddles and started knocking the ball back and forth across the net to warm up. After a few minutes, we were both ready. "Let's play a game to 21."

I said, "Okay."

We played a point to determine who would serve first. I think I served first and the game was on! Steve was pretty good. The lead went back and forth, changing many times. I led when the score reached 14 to 12.

Steve asked if I had seen the movie *The Princess Bride*.

I said, "Yes."

"Do you remember the sword fight?"

I said I had. We continued to play.

Steve got that big grin of his on his face. "I know something you don't know."

"And what is that?"

Steve confessed, "I am not left handed." And he switched his paddle from his left hand to his right.

We both laughed as we recalled and declared what a great movie and scene that it was.

The score was still close with Steve pulling ahead 18 to 16.

At this point, I said to Steve, "There is something I ought to tell you."

"Tell me," he said.

It was my turn to confess. "I am not left handed either," and I switched the paddle from my left hand to my right.

At that moment, Steve uttered the highest pitch squeal longer than any man has ever squealed: "SMIIIIIIIIIIIIIIIIIIII IIIIIIIIIIIIIIIIIIIIIIIIIIIIITH."

The children rushed into the garage to see what had happened.

"I can't believe you turned the movie around on me!"

But I did and went on to win 21-19.

We laughed some more and some more after that, about how we had exactly enacted the sword fighting scene with ping-pong paddles.

I'll never forget it.

CHAPTER 21
10-31-90

It was Halloween afternoon. I took the stand against Don Dixon. It went well. It went down well. I arrived at the courthouse shortly after lunch, which gave me plenty of time to check out the courtroom. It was the opportunity to get in and relax, see the arena, and get settled.

Steve had called me earlier in the day to tell me of his approval to go on the beeper list for a heart transplant. Six months before, he had been diagnosed with an enlarged heart. Of all the possibilities in medicine at that time, he had one and only one choice: a heart transplant. It was somewhat amazing how his approval to get on the transplant list had happened the day I would testify against Dixon. There was an ironic, non-parallel going on here. Good guy Steve develops a bad heart after saving Smith, and bad guy Dixon develops multiple crimes at Smith's expense.

Steve had given me some good suggestions about the way to act with Dixon's attorney. Simply say: *Yes, sir; No, sir; I don't understand your question, sir; I'm not finished giving my answer, sir; Would you please repeat that, sir?* Once again, Steve was right. It was like being in a judo match, the more leverage or strength you apply gives your opponent an opportunity to throw you. The more you resist, the more power you give to your opponent. I imagined I was string, allowing my opponent to push on me as much as he wanted. I offered no resistance. God bless Steve.

During the short breaks while the trial was underway, Dixon would sit cool as a cucumber reading a book, as though he was sitting in a beach chair somewhere.

I was glad to testify that day against him. Inside the courtroom, it was like I was righting the wrongs he had done to others.

I had underestimated his power as the chief manipulator. He was an unscrupulous narcissist, with the sheer ability to control those who came and went. It didn't matter who you were or what you did, he found your weakness. Somehow, he always found a way to manipulate you, always found a way to control you.

I'd realized this as I moved up through the ranks. When I got to the top, I realized that those people at the top were not any better than I'd been way down at the bottom. They too were being manipulated, Dixon's manipulation was constant because it was a total mind game with lots of money as the result. I always tried to keep my distance from Dixon, and in the end, that served me well. I had no desire to be a moth looking for the flame.

A few months later, he would find a way to manipulate the presiding judge, who gave him a questionably light sentence for the number of crimes he'd committed and was convicted of. Dixon fed the judge some reverse logic, blaming it all on the

Feds for creating an environment of loose money and easier regulations. Basically, he convinced the judge that the devil made him do it.

Alex asked me one time, "What would've happened if one of the other guys had Steve and you had their lawyer? Would you be where they are? Was it because you had a better lawyer, or were you a stronger fighter? Were you less guilty?"

It's interesting that the most culpable with a drinking problem, and the least culpable who was sober, were both given probation. The judge ruled with pity.

Every so often, sometimes years apart, God realizes you've been too comfortable. He's not messed with your life enough. He figures you need some shaking by the neck. So, he grabs you by the nape of your neck and, if you're not too woozy or too dizzy, you can sort it all out and deal with it later.

Alex continued, "What if the person who informed you of your situation over the phone had said it in a different way, you might have killed yourself. Who was with you at that time? Everyone is so different, who you're with and what you are. There are so many different variables of the possible outcomes."

Why do some people make it when everything is so seemingly against them, and why do some people just crash under the load when they seem to have everything going for them?

I think it's like an appointed time when you wake up, smell the coffee, and know that something has either changed, is changing, or about to change. Some people tune in and listen to it, others just ignore it because it's beyond them. They end up repeating the lesson over and over and over.

Some people are so into themselves, they are seriously unable to detect anything around them that involves change. It makes you wonder why.

***

Before Steve's heart issue surfaced, we were gathering files at his new office just north of Dallas. We left for lunch to talk about the future. During lunch, Steve told me he had recently had a past-life regression. Not having undergone such a session myself, I was interested in what he had to say. He described to me a time in ancient Rome when he was a judge, a cruel judge without regard for fairness, justice, or equity. Just a mean son of a bitch as he put it. He spent most of his time on an ancient bench making people's lives miserable.

He said that he was given this lifetime, the one he was living during lunch with me, to atone for the mistakes he had made in the past. His karmic challenge in this lifetime was to save me. Yes, save me from the Feds. His ruthless behavior in Roman society would be offset and forgiven if he kept me from an unjust sentence of going to prison because of Vernon Savings.

God had extended to me a lifeline through Steve, of being rescued, of him saving me from an injustice.

I had a billion questions about this, but Steve said we would have to set aside a time to explore it all in greater depth.

That time never came. Life got in the way until Steve passed away, only two years later. Having answered the bell on his karmic challenge, and having succeeded, he was done with what he came to accomplish in this lifetime. He was first diagnosed with an enlarged heart and waited patiently for a transplant, which he received. Just a few months later, he was diagnosed with pancreatic cancer and given only a few more months to live. It all happened so fast.

Many people from both sides of the judge's bench, including the FBI, would often say what a great communicator Steve Brutsché was. He was admired, even envied for his skills. He had a gift of being able to see everything at once and know what needed to be done, when and how. He liked to say, "Let's stir the ethers and shake the universe to observe reactions that point the way."

When I was struggling with the weight of criminal charges, he gave me the book *Siddhartha* to read. This was the first step for me in identifying and understanding suffering, both my own and that of others. We were both believers that if you change your world, you will change the world around you.

The day before he passed, I traveled to Dallas from Colorado to visit him. He sat in an upright chair with his back to the bedroom window. I was sitting on the floor facing him.

He said he had been in touch with his father and a friend, Brian, both of whom were on the other side. He said he was ready and knew what to expect.

I blurted, "Goddammit, how come you always know what's going to happen before I do?" I paused. "Wait a second. I take that back." I quickly retracted the dammit part I associated with God's name.

He was relaxed; he was at peace. I could see it. I could feel it. He was tired, ready to go. I thanked him for saving me and told him I would miss him. He smiled that smile and said he was supposed to. Then he said we'd see each other again.

All I have to do next is figure out my part of the pact, what I committed to do in the divine agreement he and I swore to.

CHAPTER 22
Supposed to

There he was, Don Dixon, on the evening news, again. Reclining against a white throne of hospital bed pillows, resembling the Cheshire cat impolitely disturbed from a nap. His smirk was faint, but still noticeable, as he once more told his version of the savings and loan debacle to Dallas-Fort Worth viewers, of how the federal government needed a whipping boy to bear the calamitous results that congress's deregulation had produced.

His voice gaining strength, declared that in spite of their misguided persecution, he would steadfastly carry on the fight. His wife standing at the side of his bed and attempting to smooth his sheets, strained to produce a weak smile, giving viewers the feeling that she had been prompted to do so by someone off camera.

What some people will do to get out of jail. Only weeks before, Dixon had been convicted of twenty three counts of savings and loan fraud and was caught completely unprepared for the swift handcuffing that followed the foreman's reading of the jury's verdict.

As Dixon was quickly led away by U.S. marshals, his family members sat in utter shock, disbelieving that he could be taken away. Dixon had always held the last card. Until now, he had invariably found a way to redo every deal to his satisfaction, always getting his way. But suddenly, the self-proclaimed man of invincible invisibility was on his way to prison.

It would seem that the temporary holding facility in Mansfield, Texas wouldn't be that bad for a prisoner's first-time experience. Recently completed, the facility offered a rookie environment to a rookie prisoner. But, even with its shiny floors, clean showers, and sturdy new doors, it was still the joint. Probably worse off were the unlucky guards who had been sentenced to watch him. Twenty-four hours a day, they were to make sure that Dixon's belt stayed around his waist and that his waist stayed on the ground, and not in some helicopter whisking him off to some unknown location.

Dixon commit suicide? Not a chance. Why would a guy who always had unlimited angles to everything, including angles to the angles themselves, think about giving it up now? Not even with your life.

During the second week, following his second turn down by the magistrate on his request for bond and bail appeal, Dixon developed a heart murmur. Had the realization finally set in that he was unavoidably going to reap all that he had so selfishly sown? Maybe it really is enough to give a guy a precursor to a heart attack.

What I do know is that open heart surgery got him out of the joint. But tell me, how can medical technology open his chest, repair a heart valve, and still manage to leave inside all, and I do mean all, of Don Ray Dixon's arrogance? How is it that not one tiny bit of Dixon's smugness didn't leak out somehow during surgery? What happened to the basic laws of nature? Where is the true meaning and action of osmosis? Isn't there just a tiny bit of humility moving through some semi-permeable membrane in there somewhere? Nope—not a single molecule of non-arrogance to be found anywhere.

"We will fight onward," he told viewers for the billionth time. Smugly reassuming his role as the self-appointed special victim of the Vernon Savings failure, viewers soon received a reprieve via a commercial break, wondering how a guy like this could be so delusional.

CHAPTER 23
That You, God?

During my life, this life, I've been spared from death a number of times. Each event coming close to my not being here anymore, I would think to myself, why didn't I die? I have no doubt that Guardian Angels and Guides actually exist, and I believe each person has more than one. I vividly remember four times I should have been dead.

In the first event, I was a third grader hanging out with an older kid, maybe a sixth grader, near Madison Elementary in Oklahoma City. There was a large creek northeast of the school, where a construction company had dumped a good deal of concrete chunks with protruding rebar on the side of the creek sloping away from where we stood. We decided to cross the creek using the concrete as a bridge, with the older kid going first using bigger steps to land on the largest concrete pieces. I was next. He said to go slow and watch out for the rebar, which was twisted and protruding in weird angles from the concrete chunks.

After only a few steps, I tripped and began to tumble head over heels. I couldn't tell where to place my hands or my feet to avoid the deadly rebar sticking out like a mine field.

Finally, I came to a stop, uninjured at the bottom of the slope near the water.

My new friend said, "I don't believe you just did that."

"Did what?"

He shook his head. "There's no way you should have gotten through that much crooked steel without mangling yourself on the tangled rebar. I don't believe that I just saw what I saw."

I didn't have much of a reply to what he was saying. But I didn't feel a presence. It was growing dark so we decided to split up. I crossed over the creek and headed towards home, wondering why I wasn't hurt, grateful but not sure how, feeling a calmness around me.

***

When I was a fifth grader, because Daddy needed an extended stay at the mental hospital, we could no longer afford the white stone house we lived in. It was sold, and we moved into another house in Buchanan Elementary District. I went from being a Magpie to a Bruin.

One day after a heavy rain, I took my dog Poncho, a mid-size Airedale-poodle mix, for a walk toward 10th Street. A concrete canal with slanted side walls was nearly full of rainwater, rushing through it at a pretty high speed. I got the idea to jump in for a brief ride and get out before the canal went under the street about 50 yards away. So, I jumped.

The rainwater was moving faster than I had thought, and it was now in charge of me and my plan. I could not get to the side walls to get out. I was trapped in the canal's center where the water was fastest.

On a dry day, I had previously explored the canal, walking to the end, it opened at ground level where a landscape business was located. Moving rapidly as I approached the road with the rainwater accelerating under it, I saw the opening was only about a foot high between the water and the road. I realized if I went under, I wouldn't come out alive.

Reaching the side of the road above, I threw up my arms to grab the sidewalk and avoid being pulled under. Then, I realized problem number two. The runaway rainwater pulling my legs was stronger than my skinny arms hugging the road. After a few minutes, my arms began to slip, I was losing my grip. I struggled harder, but to no avail.

All of a sudden, I felt a tug at the end of my right shirt sleeve. It was Poncho. He had grabbed ahold of my shirt with chomped teeth, pulling on all fours, making backward thrusts. It was just enough to enable me to move to the side where the water wasn't so fast, and crawl away from the canal. I was spent.

Poncho sat next to me until I could get up. Then, we headed home probably accompanied by a few of my Guardian Angels.

***

A couple of years later, I attended Taft Junior High in Oklahoma City. I saw the principal, Mr. Turner, so often for paddlings that he invited me to join him, a counselor, and two other seventh-grade students for a camping trip to New Mexico during spring break. My parents said okay.

It was an okay trip, even though the other two boys were kind of dull and unfriendly. So, what's new?

On the way back through the national forest on a two lane highway, we were approaching a steep hairpin curve going up and to the left. As we began our ascent, a black Porsche appeared at the top of the curve and attempted the steep curve without slowing. It's a Porsche, right?

I had been sitting in the seat behind Mr. Turner, to his right, so I could see where we were going. I had a good view of the Porsche coming at us.

The Porsche couldn't handle the turn on the snow and ice and slid sideways, down toward us, finally meeting us pretty much head on.

We met at the bottom of the curve. The noise from the crash was loud. Not only from the two vehicles meeting metal, but the camping gear transferring itself from the back of Mr. Turner's white station wagon to the front.

The tent polls had been placed in the back of the station wagon and, upon the cars colliding, fired themselves forward toward the windshield. In surveying the damage, we determined that four of the tent poles shot by me like long, bulleted spears, two to the left of my neck and two to the right about an inch from my ear. The counselor said, "Johnny, you are one lucky kid." Once again, I felt a calm presence.

***

I was in Vietnam in 1968 and 1969. When the monsoon was ending in '68, I transferred to a Chinook company, moving to the other side of the metal tarmac. Phu Loi was the army airfield between Saigon and Tay Ninh West. Rocket and mortar fire were common and sometimes accurately aimed by the Viet Cong.

I settled in with my new company and had about 90 days left, qualifying me as a short timer. During an early March morning attack, we were awakened to two rocket explosions with the sirens going off.

Later that morning in the mess hall, I overheard talk about where the rockets had landed. They were pointing to an area next to my hooch, making an arc with their hands for where it came from and how it came in.

I was surprised to learn that we had taken some shrapnel in my part of the hooch. I went back to check things out and talked to a couple of guys who bunked near me. They were pointing out the areas where the shrapnel passed through near their bunks.

When they left, I went back to my bunk and began searching for shrapnel and holes. I discovered a row of small, jagged holes forming a bumpy line about two feet above my bed. I could see it hadn't missed by much. I stepped outside to view where the shrapnel entered from the outside. I went back in to look again. The shrapnel holes were still there.

My curiosity confirmed a presence once again. I wondered how many other close calls had already occurred that I didn't know about. And how many more would occur until I arrived stateside. God works in mysterious ways. Thanks God!

CHAPTER 24
Front Page News

After receiving an early release from probation in 1991, we moved to Breckenridge, Colorado to manage a condo hotel lodge, and to protect a family investment made by Alex's father. Using some basic auditing techniques, I had discovered that the management company he had hired was stealing from him in every way imaginable. So, we soon found ourselves as the new managers.

During the next few years, we moved frequently in Breckenridge, renting our houses to take advantage of the prices that ski season tourists would pay. We soon made an offer to Alex's father to buy him out. He accepted payments monthly over time.

I began a small upper end townhome development in 1994, where I also built a new home for us. In 1995, we began selling the condos at the condo hotel to individual buyers, and created a homeowners' association, as well as a management company to manage it and the short-term rental contracts for the new owners. During these years, I became active in the community of Breckenridge and Summit County. I joined the Summit County Rotary Club and became a Paul Harris Fellow. I interviewed and was appointed to the Board of Directors of the Summit County Housing Authority, joining the effort to provide housing for low-income residents, which had been and still is an ongoing problem. In 1993, I ran for and was elected to the Board of Directors of the Summit County School District. I served as a school board member until November 1995, when I was "de-elected" as a result of a newspaper article that was printed about my involvement in Vernon Savings.

The article was printed on the last day that the local newspaper was in business, by the publisher/editor who had contacted me regarding Vernon Savings a few days before. He had received an anonymous tip, researched and confirmed it with the *Dallas Morning News*, and wanted my statement. The headline screamed across the top of the front page "School Board Member Admits Felony Guilty Plea." The article below was the full front page, giving new meaning to local sensationalism.

The next day, the other local newspapers ran articles, not wanting to miss out on printing their own version of the scandal. That weekend, my Rotary club held a scheduled health management event at the middle school in Frisco. I arrived to take care of the booth assignments I had signed up for, not knowing I would be Mr. Front Page a few days before. I remember one of the County Commissioners approaching me, asking, "What are you doing here?" I said, "I signed up to help out." He looked at me with a pensive sort of look and said, "I don't know you that well, but I do know it took a lot of guts for you to be here today." I answered, "It's either come here or find a rock big enough to crawl under."

During the ensuing months, I did basically crawl under the rock I spoke about, by moving my family to the front range. We chose Lafayette, Colorado, a town next to Boulder, where I built another home. I made a feeble attempt at Rotary there, but didn't have the heart for it. I was afraid that the next day would be the one when I would be found out again.

CHAPTER 25
Plane Crash

When Woody got out of prison in 1993-1994, Junior said some unkind words about Woody that friends of Woody didn't appreciate. There was an upcoming golf tournament they were all in, and a few people wondered if Woody was going to hit Junior or what.

Junior always had a drinking problem. Sometimes it led to him running off at the mouth. But it also caused the judge to give him more leniency in his sentence. I hope he's got a handle on his drinking problem now.

But Woody was a guy who didn't hold a grudge with anybody and was not bitter. He had a kind of charisma that made you want to make sure that the horse you bet on was the same horse Woody bet on. If others bet against him, they'd sure regret, it because they always lost. He was good at dominoes, cards, and dice, and usually won against would-be takers. He liked his aces, straights, and flushes. People never learned.

He was a regular small-town guy who got caught up in the euphoria of what was going on at Vernon Savings. But, he was still a deal guy, and super smart in that respect—wheeler-dealer Woody. He was the brains of the banking operation and Dixon had to have him. The hooks ran deep with Dixon. In the end, Woody had dealt himself a situation that he couldn't get out of.

Woody shouldn't have been given a thirty-year sentence. He turned down a deal for five, and he probably would have gotten five to ten years. He was willing to pay his debt to society like a man instead of screaming and kicking and yelling like some of the others. Woody was remorseful. He wished things had been different, that he had gone down a different path. Later, his sentence was reduced to five years, and he served three before returning to Vernon.

At least Woody came out with money in his pocket. Most people were completely wiped out, but not Woody. He had positioned himself well; he was a shrewd guy.

There was a time when Woody was the guy in Vernon, Texas, who people thought walked on water.

Vernon High had a pretty good football team back then. They went to state and lost the first time. The next year they went to state and won. I went to a playoff game at Texas Stadium in Irving outside of Dallas.

I wasn't sure which side I should sit on, not knowing which side was Vernon's, so I walked part way down the steps. It didn't take me long to figure out where the Vernon people were: almost everyone was wearing a Rolex. That was the Vernon side.

The employees of Vernon Savings thought they were doing so well, thinking they were lucky to be part of the economic pride. The same as what the people in Dallas thought. What a masquerade. No one knew what damage Dixon had done.

When I was living in Lafayette outside of Boulder, FBI Agent Hogue called me on a Monday in May 1998. We visited for a bit, then he said the purpose of his call was to tell me that Woody had died in a plane crash.

Wow! What a shock! Not only Woody, but his wife Paula and his mother had died in the crash, too. Paula was the pilot. They were leaving from Vernon for Austin, where Woody's nephew was in the state finals for the shotput. What a tragic ending. A mechanical problem had caused the plane to go down. Just after take off, one of the engines started cutting out.

A friend of Paula, who'd taught her how to fly, was on the ground in radio contact and gave her instructions on what to do. He told her to take the plane around and land it in the wheat field.

Paula replied, "NO! I just bought this plane. I'll bring it around, bring it right back. I'm not landing in a wheat field. I'm bringing this plane back to the airport!"

A friend of Woody's and the family declared Paula to be "the most stubborn woman that I have ever been around in my lifetime."

Speculation is that she cut the engine to restart and banked around over the Altus Highway north of town. The plane was full of fuel, the weight kicked in and drove the plane into the highway where it exploded.

I'm told you never bank or make a turn into a dead engine. It's obvious that she had never been in that situation, or any type of situation like it. She was known as a pretty good pilot. But it was a bad outcome.

Agent Hogue and I talked about Woody and the days of Vernon Savings for quite a long time. I could tell that even though he had prosecuted Woody, he had a great deal of respect for him. At least more than any of the other defendants maybe, except for me.

Dixon was at the funeral, wearing gold chains and his shirt open. The collective thought that it took a lot of balls for Dixon to be there. But he was from Vernon, too.

Agent Hogue and I said our goodbyes, wondering when the next Vernon Savings issue would arise that would require his input and my testimony. Turns out, it wasn't too much longer after that phone conversation, that we met again, three years later at yet another federal courtroom in Dallas.

CHAPTER 26
Rickie Wayne

In 1999, I heard that Rick Ramsey was in the hospital and had been there a short while. He wasn't doing very well and had undergone some surgeries. Apparently, they found cancer in the frontal part of his brain behind his facial mask.

I got the information from his son Scott, and told Scott that I'd like to go by and see his dad. He was glad that I'd called, and asked me to do that.

Alex and I arrived, walked to the door of his room, and met up with Scott. He said Rick had not been very active and was sleeping most of the time.

Upon my speaking, Rick heard my voice and woke up. Later, Scott told me that Rick had been out of it for a couple of days, not really communicating with anyone. Scott was quite surprised that Rick reacted the way he did. He said I could speak with Rick, but I would have to stand very close to position my ear near his mouth.

As I did that, Rick began talking nonstop. He was telling me various things in earnest with a new energy.

I hate to say it, but I didn't understand much of Rick's garbled words. From the rapid pace and anxiety in his voice, I sensed he was scared of dying.

With a calm voice, I told him not to be scared, that heaven was waiting on him because he had earned a place. He was a Church of Christ guy and had played the part well.

CHAPTER 27
FBI Lunch

In my 14th year of working with the FBI, I got a phone call again from FBI Agent Hogue in charge of all Vernon Savings cases. He asked if I could meet him for lunch in Bedford. Over the years, we had become friends and respected each other. The waitress seated us and served us iced tea.

It had not been long since we were reunited in a federal income tax case filed by Woody's estate. He began by saying he had been in touch with all the others who had been involved in the prosecutions of Vernon Savings individuals. He said he had confirmed with all agents, and both of the Justice Department attorneys who prosecuted my case. He paused, then said, "They all were in agreement and wanted you to know, John, that we should not have prosecuted you."

I was stunned. It took a few minutes to gather my composure. When I could breathe and talk at the same time, I looked at him and said with a shaky voice, "Looks like you're buying lunch."

He went on to say that they wanted to encourage me to make an application for a Presidential Pardon. He said they didn't know much about the process, but they would support it.

I thought about making the application and talked with Alex and my best friend Coach. I learned that it would be something like what our friend Yogi Berra used to say: "It's gonna be *Deja vu* all over again." It meant that we would be questioned and interviewed by the FBI on behalf of the Pardon Attorney's Office. Once again, my family, friends, employees, business associates, neighbors, and only God and the FBI knew who else, would be involved in a new investigation.

I put it off for almost a year. One day I was talking to Coach on the phone, we were going over the application filing again, and he said with a pleading voice, "Hey man, you gotta do it. You just got to do it."

Soon after that telephone conversation, and talking it over with Alex again, I decided to make the application. I did not hire an attorney to make the application for me. I obtained the application form from the Pardon Attorney's office in Washington DC. I prepared requested information for their review. I remember looking for a typewriter, because I had two choices: one was to print it by hand and the other was to type it. It took me a lot longer than I thought to find a regular old typewriter, but I finally found one on the Internet.

With the embarrassing newspaper article from 1995 still fresh in my mind, I thought about how that continued to make me hesitate to be more involved in the community.

I enclosed a copy of a letter that I wrote to the Department of Justice attorneys last January, updating them on what I had been doing for the past 15 years as Exhibit "A." I described my experience as a Summit County, Colorado School Board Member as an example of just how difficult it is to participate actively in community affairs when you carry the stigma of a felony conviction.

I enclosed a copy of the newspaper article concerning the public embarrassment as a school board member as Exhibit "C". I also enclosed as Exhibit "D" a page from an application form for volunteer work at Cook's Children's Hospital in Fort Worth, Texas reflecting disclosure of previous felony convictions, and an article from the *Wall Street Journal* as Exhibit "E" discussing the same. I also enclosed as Exhibit "F" *Parade Magazine's* cover concerning a call to volunteer service by President Bush.

I wanted once again to become active in my community as a volunteer in various charitable programs, explore the possibility of running for a seat on the local school board, join the local Rotary Club, and expand my efforts of providing affordable housing to include the raising of funds from outside sources, that would most certainly require detailed disclosures of my background.

With the everyday news of corporate/financial fraud and deception, I knew I had a message that should again be heard, especially by those in college who will be our business leaders of the future. I often thought about opening myself up and sharing my experiences again, but the thought of scandal and the impact on my family had kept me quiet. Having a Presidential Pardon would lessen the stigma of my felony conviction and would serve to propel me back to the podium.

I also attached as Exhibit "B" a letter from Steven Learned, Attorney for the Department of Justice, stating his willingness to assist in this application for Presidential Pardon.

I stated in my application that over the years, I had tried to right the wrong that I caused at Vernon Savings and Loan, through testifying for the United States Department of Justice and by giving speeches on the topic of ethics. For 14 years, I had been the key witness for the Department of Justice, testifying numerous times in both criminal and civil cases. I was told by the Department of Justice that my cooperation and testimony saved the Federal Government millions of dollars and countless hours of time.

Since the beginning weeks of the investigation of Vernon Savings and Loan, I tried in every way possible to right my crime and to be a responsible, productive citizen. I sincerely regretted that my actions, including my lack of proper action, caused problems, heartaches, and pain for others.

I completed and sent in my application for presidential pardon in December 2003.

Each year during the week of Thanksgiving, I would call the office in Washington DC to speak with the pardon attorney, Hope McGowan, who had been assigned to my case. Each year, I began the conversation by saying, "I've seen the turkeys again on TV getting a pardon from the President for Thanksgiving. Just checking to see if my application is still under consideration."

Each year she would reply, "Mr. Smith, I'm unable to give you any information with respect to your pardon application."

"Yes, I know, just trying to see if it's been thrown away or if you might still be working on it."

"I have said all I can say, Mr. Smith."

"I know, I know. Thanks again."

CHAPTER 28
Nazis for Neighbors

In June of 2006, we moved back to Colorado and bought a house on a corner lot on Nelson St. in Littleton. One evening, I was picking up dog droppings in the backyard and met the daughter-in-law of the elderly lady living next door.

During our conversation she told me, among other things, that most of the family, including her husband, worked for the Sheriff's department.

My bag was now full and I said, "Nice to meet you. Hope to see you again."

In parting, she said that if we ever needed help from the law, to contact them, that they would be glad to help us in some way.

Alex and I started our usual routine of deciding what we wanted to upgrade. This house was located on a corner lot, and a tract home, so it needed a lot. In September, we put in a side fence between us and the house next door. The location of the fence, just inside our property line, revealed that a white PVC pipe coming from next door was encroaching onto our property.

Since her elderly mother-in-law lived there, I decided not to bother her with the matter. Later that fall, the elderly lady passed away.

I met her son across the side fence and offered my condolences. While talking, I noticed the pipe and asked him if he knew what it was. He said he didn't, but would take care of it.

Some months passed, and I saw a For Sale sign in the neighbor's front yard. I called the real estate agent to get contact information for the seller. I informed the agent of the pipe trespassing onto my property and that it was discharging water onto my property. The real estate agent was not aware of the pipe and said she would contact the seller.

After not hearing from anyone about the pipe for a few days, I elevated the end of the pipe on my property 30-40 degrees to demonstrate that the water was discharging from the pipe onto my property. The next morning, I could see an icicle on the lower lip of the pipe, which showed that water continued to discharge onto my property.

In March, I left for business in Texas and returned the next week. I discovered that the pipe had been cut and removed from my property, but it was still aimed at my property. I went to the Jefferson County Building Code Enforcement Department and was told that although it was improper, they couldn't do anything about it. I spoke with County zoning enforcement, who said they were unable to do anything and that it was a civil matter.

I called the real estate agent and told her that just cutting the pipe wasn't enough and that the pipe was still discharging water onto my property. She argued that the builder designed the drainage that way. I told her that I didn't want to argue and said, "I guess I'll have to call my attorney."

She replied, "Go for it."

At 8:30 the next morning my doorbell rang. I opened the door to find a middle age woman in a Sheriff's uniform standing on my front porch. She introduced herself as a deputy from Jefferson County, and asked if I was having some issues with a pipe. Not thinking why she would be there asking that question, I said, "Sure. Follow me."

We went through the house and outside to the area between the two houses and I explained all that had happened.

During my explanation, she interrupted me and asked, "Did you touch the pipe?"

I said, "Yes, I wanted to demonstrate that it was discharging water onto my property."

She then said, "You're under arrest and, accordingly, I am going to have to issue you a ticket for criminal mischief."

Not believing that any of this was actually happening, I restated the facts to no avail; my words fell upon two deaf ears. The pipe was on my property without permission I reiterated, I didn't damage or deface anything!

Completely ignoring what I was saying, she handed me a summons for criminal mischief and explained that I now had an upcoming hearing date. Then she left.

I was pissed, but mostly in shock. During the next few weeks I fumed aloud, "Why is this happening to me? How in the world can I expect a Presidential Pardon after another conviction?"

Finally, I remembered the words from the daughter-in-law next door: "If you need the law, just let us know."

When that memory came, I realized I had been set up and framed! My next door "neighbor" had called in one of their Jeffco deputy friends to stop me in my tracks with the charge of criminal mischief. Utterly preposterous!

Now I really knew how Job felt, and I also knew that he had infinitely more patience. I screamed openly toward the sky, "This is the United States of America! This isn't supposed to happen here! Am I reliving a previous life for some karmic lesson I have not yet settled? Have I not sacrifice the right number of goats? What caused this to happen? Have I once again been abandoned? What wrong have I done to deserve this? Don't you realize that I have a pending application with the United States government for a Presidential Pardon? Does this mean, nice try, Johnny, you've come up short again, just as you headed down the home stretch? Stepped on your dick again, didn't you John Boy? You can't seem to get out of your own way." I kept asking myself, without an answer, an infamous question, "Father, why hast thou forsaken me?"

Over the next few weeks, I replayed in my head the issue and the ticket-issuing scene. Unbelievably, I found myself once again having to find a lawyer.

One of my first conversations was with a battle-scarred lawyer. It was her opinion that our approach should pretty much be to strap on the gun belts and grenades to shove this egregious matter back in the face of the county Sheriff's department. After listening to her strategy, I thought that someone with an apparent grudge should not be leading our cause.

Having learned about lawyers and criminal matters, this was not the path to take. Headlines were the last thing I should try to create, especially if I didn't want to disturb the Justice Department and the Pardon Attorney's Office.

After a week or so, I found an attorney who had been a deputy district attorney for Jefferson County. This was the right person, because he understood the psychology and mentality that lived in the shadows within the county criminal system.

Having been falsely accused, who knew when the Gestapo would come knocking again or be lurking around the corner to charge us with something else? We were in a situation where we did not know what to expect next. We were unable to trust our own authorities. When we saw a black and white JeffCo Sherriff's car, we held our breath.

During our first meeting with the deputy district attorney, our attorney provided her a letter of confidential plea bargain correspondence, and explained the facts of the events. I had hoped that she would view what had happened as purposely contrived.

NO! It didn't faze her, not even a little bit.

We gritted our teeth while my case moved slowly towards disposition. I kept telling Alex, "This is a test. We're being tested. We can't throw in the towel now. Gotta hang tough! It's just more karma coming back at us. What the hell did we do to deserve this?"

As my criminal mischief case made its way to the county judge, his response after reading the information put forth was, "Are you kidding?" Shortly thereafter, my case was dismissed.

My confidence in the criminal system, which I had learned the hard way, had been sorely shaken. However, my application for Presidential Pardon remained in place and undisturbed. Can we just wait this one out, oh Lord? Who knows how long it will be for the result to come? We have no idea when. No more tricks or tests. We've suffered enough. Okay?

CHAPTER 29
There's Always Hope

It was a Monday morning on December 10, 2007 just after Pearl Harbor day. I was in the kitchen in Littleton, the same kitchen I had escorted the Sheriff's deputy through to view the pipe. It had been four months since my unlawful arrest was finally laid to rest and sealed. I continued to wait patiently for the Presidential Pardon, not knowing how many more years I would have to wait.

The phone rang. I picked it up. I said hello.

"Good morning, Mr. Smith. This is Hope McGowan from the U.S. Pardon Attorney's office. I'm calling to inform you that President Bush has granted you a presidential pardon and wishes you a Merry Christmas."

I said, simply, "Thank you, and please thank the President for me."

We said goodbye.

I hung up the phone and my legs gave out on me. I slipped to the floor. I was overwhelmed. I began to sob for release and maybe happiness. Almost as much as the boy sobbed a long time ago at Pap and Mammy's.

Thanks again, Mr. President!

CHAPTER 30
Integrity-Resentment

My experience is, you have to have awareness before you can develop or exercise your consciousness. You have to know what's happening and what's not happening. Are there issues to deal with? Are there issues involving ethics? I thought I could be instrumental in spreading integrity, that people looked up to integrity, that people regarded integrity as something they wanted to have.

I partnered with a man in San Diego to create a website on the topic. He had written a book on the subject, and the website would be a vehicle not only to post his book, but also to present to the public other information and definitions about integrity. What I learned from my participation, is that people don't care about integrity, because people already think they have integrity and that everybody else has it, too.

I would give a twenty-minute speech on integrity to Rotary members, and get a standing ovation, and then nothing would come from it. Not another booking, not another speech, not another anything. Not even a question. They would pack up all the integrity they knew they already had and go home.

For me, what I felt inside about what had happened at Vernon Savings was an ongoing emotional project. The boy knew what we felt inside. What I'm still feeling, churning deep inside, is that the anger machine is still there and it has become even angrier. I've learned that anger and grief are first cousins, not traveling far without each other. I was chosen to be prosecuted by circumstance, by association. I'm left with deep resentment and anguish for what transpired.

I don't resent the people who gave me the opportunity to cross the Rubicon. I don't resent the friends that I made, the FBI agents, nor the Justice Department attorneys. I don't resent any of them for what they did in prosecuting me. They just did their jobs.

My resentment goes to Dixon, Woody, the other executive officers—especially loan officers—who knew what was going down. They were all in for themselves. They couldn't care less about the people who were affected, their careers ruined or lessened. They didn't care about a guy like me. They probably thought I knew as much as they did, that's how Dixon worked. Those guys, I'm still angry with them, I still resent what they did.

Fifteen years after my conviction, I remember a session break outside a federal courtroom where Woody's estate was making claims against the government on money unfairly taxed. I sat on a bench out in the hallway that faced another bench, upon which were Junior and the Phantom. They were laughing, joking, and slapping their thighs as they recalled the Vernon Savings days. From their loud antics, you would never know what those guys had caused, and what they had gone through as a result. You wouldn't think of them as having lost anything;

maybe they did, but you couldn't tell. I'm told the Phantom was prosecuted and served time in a penitentiary in Florida.

I thought about what I had lost: a career, professional status, reputation, my integrity. Not caring if they were disruptive, they struck me as a couple of clowns: void of conscience without regard for their impact on others.

Even today, a Monday in 2017, I still carry the resentment of what happened, and what happened to me.

CHAPTER 31
Inner Peace

I don't think there is any doubt that I should be at the front of the line for learning how to achieve inner peace. The grief I endured from the events in the past is still present, and sometimes overwhelmingly present.

The Peace Pilgrim was a woman who had abandoned personal possessions and walked over 25,000 miles for peace, until her death in 1981. The Peace Pilgrim guided Steve in the last few years of his life, particularly in his career from litigation to establishing mediation in the state of Texas, and ultimately beyond that in finding his higher self. Below is a summary of the Steps of Inner Peace from the Peace Pilgrim.

FOUR PREPARATIONS:

1. Assume right attitude toward life.

Stop being an escapist or a surface-liver, as these attitudes can only cause disharmony in your life. Face life squarely and get down below the froth, below the surface to discover its verities and realities. Solve the problems that life sets before you, and you will find that solving them contributes to your inner growth. Helping to solve collective problems contributes also to your growth, and these problems should never be avoided.

2. Live good beliefs.

The laws governing human conduct apply as rigidly as the law of gravity. Obedience to these laws pushes us toward harmony; disobedience pushes us toward disharmony. Since many of these laws are already common belief, you can begin by putting into practice all the good things you believe. No life can be in harmony unless belief and practice are in harmony.

3. Find your place in the Life Pattern.

You have a part in the scheme of things. What that part is you can know only from within yourself. You can seek it in receptive silence. You can begin to live in accordance with it by doing all the good things you are motivated toward and giving these things priority in your life over all the superficial things that customarily occupy human lives.

4. Simplify life to bring inner and outer wellbeing into harmony.

Unnecessary possessions are unnecessary burdens. Many lives are cluttered not only with unnecessary possessions but also with meaningless activities. Cluttered lives are out-of-harmony lives and require simplification. Wants and needs can become the same in a human life and, when this is accomplished, there will be a sense of harmony between inner and outer well-being. Such harmony is needful not only in the individual life but in the collective life, too.

FOUR PURIFICATIONS:

1. Purification of the bodily temple.

Are you free from all bad habits? In your diet do you stress the vital foods—the fruits, whole grains, vegetables, and nuts? Do you get to bed early and get enough sleep? Do you get plenty of fresh air, sunshine, exercise, and contact with nature? If you can answer yes to these questions, you have gone a long way toward purification of the bodily temple

2. Purification of the thoughts.

It is not enough to do right things and say right things. You must also *think* right things. Positive thoughts can be powerful influences for good. Negative thoughts can make you physically ill. Be sure there is no unpeaceful situation between yourself and any other human being, for only when you have ceased to harbor unkind thoughts can you attain inner harmony.

3. Purification of the desires.

Since you are here to get yourself into harmony with the laws that govern human conduct and with your part in the scheme of things, your desires should be focused in this direction.

4. Purification of motives.

Obviously, your motive should never be greed or self-seeking, or the wish for self-glorification, you shouldn't even have the selfish motive of attaining inner peace for yourself. Being of service to your fellow humans must be your motive before your life can come into harmony.

FOUR RELINQUISHMENTS:

1. Relinquishment of self-will.

You have, or it's as though you have, two selves: the lower self that usually governs you selfishly, and the higher self which stands ready to use you gloriously. You must subordinate the lower self by refraining from doing the not-good things you are motivated toward, not suppressing them but transforming them so that the higher self can take over your life

2. Relinquishment of the feeling of separateness.

All of us, all over the world, are cells in the body of humanity. You are not separate from your fellow humans, and you cannot find harmony for yourself alone. You can only find harmony when you realize the oneness of all and work for the good of all.

3. Relinquishment of attachments.

Only when you have relinquished all attachments can you be really free. Material things are here for use, and anything you cannot relinquish when it has outlived its usefulness possesses you. You can only live in harmony with your fellow humans if you have no feeling that you possess them, and therefore do not try to run their lives.

4. Relinquishment of all negative feelings.

Work on relinquishing negative feelings. If you live in the present moment, which is really the only moment you have to live, you will be less apt to worry. If you realize that those who do mean things are psychologically ill, your feelings of anger will turn to feelings of pity. If you recognize that all of your inner hurts are caused by your own wrong actions or your own wrong reactions or your own wrong inaction, then you will stop hurting yourself.

CHAPTER 32
For Your Pocket

I see the date and wonder how this much time could have already passed. It seems as though it all just happened yesterday. Even though I curse myself again and again to stop thinking about it, to forget it, I still get this ticky, time warp feeling whenever I realize that I've drifted back into reliving yet another scene of the Vernon Savings debacle, and the Justice Department experience that followed.

Sometimes, I discover myself in an endless loop of peeling through the whys and wherefores of it all, but the re-sorting never seems to be able to produce a different ending.

Other times, I'm guilty of attempting to mentally alter the outcome, so that not so many had their lives so assuredly shattered.

Finally, I find some consolation in imagining that given the opportunity of time travel, I would return to accurately detect the smoke and mirrors for what they really were. Galloping up and down the halls of the corporate offices like Paul Revere, I'd call out for all to hear: "Wake up! Wake up! The nightmare is coming. This isn't real, it's a dream, wake up!"

Since leaving the S&L, time has traveled onward, marching its way up and down me, inflicting its lessons upon me, regardless of whether I was prepared for them or not.

Fortunately, my most important lesson was learned early on—it led to my developing a very special relationship with the word pretense. Hating it, coming to grips with it, acknowledging it so it would loosen its hold over me, I was then allowed to forge new conclusions, conclusions filled with cavernous discrepancies, between what we thought we were at Vernon Savings and what we turned out to be.

Don't blindly believe in your superiors. Use your own judgment. You know, your own gut feeling. You know those times you told yourself to do something you didn't do, and the voice said you should have done it. The same voice that whispered to you that you have been involved in too many situational ethics decisions. Listen to it. That's your training. That's the voice of your intuition; remember that awareness leads to consciousness.

When you play ethics games, you argue one way in one situation, and when you walk into the next situation, you argue them differently because of the situation. The little voice is the one that's going to tell you, "Hey, you're being a little selective in your memory about who's doing what; you're looking down, looking in this direction, but maybe you ought to be looking around more; hey, is there something really going on here?" Listen to yourself. Ask yourself: do these people really know more than I do? In what way do things seem to be here?

What are some of the signs to look for?

Communication. How well does this group communicate?

At Vernon Savings, they communicated in pockets. The managerial style was never for everyone to know what was going on. It was always for one group to know this, and one group to know that. And if you were lucky, you might have bumped into one guy from one group on your way down the hall for a drink of water, and the next guy from the other group on the way back from the bathroom. So, you could find out what was going on, but only if you were in the right place at the right time, and only if you put effort into it.

A decentralized management structure that is dominated from the top. At the top of Vernon Savings was where all the moths were. The flame was the owner and all the moths were the ministers who wanted to get near the flame and be part of it. Of course, they were blinded by it and eventually got singed. And they were all brought in individually.

The Board of Directors in Vernon, Texas consisted of a lot of people who were over 65 years old. They thought they were great to be a part of Vernon Savings. They would elbow each other in the ribs so they could second the motion on approving loans they knew absolutely nothing about. Some loan officer would stand up and say, "We're going to do this loan in Florida, it's a great loan." And they'd go "Aye, aye!" just to be part of this wonderful, moneymaking rocket ship called Vernon Savings. Executive committees? Oh, they had existed in a floating kind of way among two or three people. Managerial weakness, look for that.

Someone asked me, "When you recognized it, how would you have changed it?" At first I thought, you know, I don't know if I could have changed it. Because something like that is already created; it is already fashioned. That's the house and, if you want to live there, you have to live there. What do you do about it? You go get another job. That's what you do about it. You get up and you leave. Or if you're a public accountant, you go get another client. There are plenty of clients out there. There are plenty of jobs out there, too.

The COO was the former deputy commissioner of the Texas savings-and-loan commission. He was not the owner. He was not an unscrupulous individual. But he ended up much like I did. Yes, the money was great. Yes, the money was powerful. Over a period of years, there were a number of high quality people hired at top levels of Vernon Savings. It was always my opinion that we had good people there. Good people who knew what they were doing. Good, this thing is going to be run right. Good, this thing is not going to have a problem. I don't have to worry about the things that I had to worry about once upon a time.

It was like when I was in Nam. If you really were going to make it home, you never thought you would be one of the guys that wasn't going to make it back.

CHAPTER 33
The Future

Steve liked to present the two of us as a brotherhood, for we understood certain things that other people did not. We were both big believers in integrity. "What was lost is now found," he would often say. Still, as the lawyer that he was in this lifetime, his view of this book's last chapter, was that it should be one of summation. *Get out your best closing argument John Boy, for you are reliving now what you were accused of. I have the answer. The words. You should trust your own words.*

Steve describes the part where he, the teacher, hands off to me the student. He wants to step aside with his hand on my shoulder for my words to come forth. Our lives have been a living testimony to integrity. There's never been a greater time in history, when what people say and what people do stand in such stark contrast. Are they the same? Saying one thing and doing another? Living what you preach or not?

What do you think about that? Steve asked. As we both knew, I have had a huge issue with trust. A clinging indignation results from those I trusted when I shouldn't have. My anger machine is still close by; grief and anger are still inseparable at times. Sometimes, I'm unable to tell which one is which. But, in spite of that, I am still able to hear Steve's advice to me:

Be confident and trust yourself. Be careful not to over complicate things. Integrity is simply putting words into action;

what you say and the conduct that follows. Your message will reach many audiences. It will reach people and they will relate to integrity explained as "what you say and what you do." Your version of integrity, the message, is different and will reach people, those who I would not have thought would be interested. People want integrity; they just don't know what it is. Can you not see how far your great impact will travel?

True, this message has not been gifted or given before. What's cool is that I will reach people who have not been reached before.

You will blow apart the stereotype! Wow, that's so awesome, he says, using the word "stoked," which I haven't heard in a while. Feels really good. He wants me to find the passion that he has. He wants me to take leaps of faith in what I am doing.

Just put it out there and trust. I know what I'm doing, he says.

I recall the times when Mama said that I showed them. "You showed them then and you're showing them now, Johnny."

There were plenty of doubters, people who didn't believe in me. But I showed them, I'm showing them now. It's my turn.

You did it! You did it! Give yourself some credit. It wasn't just my doing—it took the both of us to get it done.

I know.

I persevered, I did my part to succeed and ultimately was granted a Presidential Pardon by President George Bush. But, it's as though I'm still bemoaning what had happened to me. I still seem to be hanging on to the lesson, still kicking myself in the butt for letting it happen.

It's only a lesson Johnny, not a life sentence. Mama's team from the other side say it's not about the why any more, it's no longer about the why. It's now all about getting and giving your message.

Living my truth, getting and having meaning in my life. What can we learn from continued grief? What is the purpose of that?

I'm trying to make sense of it, but it doesn't make sense. I'm trying to make it okay. But what happened wasn't okay. What does matter is how I choose to live life now and what I'm choosing now. That's what matters.

Yes, that's the lesson! The lesson isn't the act: it's what you did or have done with the act.

Steve always did say I was stubborn. My usual reply was, "What am I being stubborn about now?" This time he answers:

It's about letting it go, letting go of your wanting to know the why. What matters now is that wrongs can be righted by how you live your life.

He's pained that I still, to this day, give power to those who caused the misfortune, as I chase the why. I realize now that it is not serving me anymore and that soon, I will leave it behind as I evolve through it.

In looking back, I can see that the Federal government had opened the door to the perfect storm. I cannot right a wrong that wasn't mine. Yet, I have righted my voice and a message of integrity. I choose to be an advocate, a voice for integrity- simple integrity. It is what I believe I am called to do.

APPENDIX I
The Communicator

As stated previously, many people from both sides of the judge's bench, including the Justice Department, would say to themselves, what a great communicator Steve Brutsché was. He was admired, even envied for his skills. He had a gift of being able to see everything at once and know what needed to be done, when and how.

Steve wrote many papers, standards and guidelines for mediation, negotiation, and communication in general. Below is one of his writings on communication that we can all learn from.

The Art of Successful Communication

Successful communication results from the combined efforts of the speaker and the listener. The speaker attempts to transmit an intended message, which is received and interpreted by the listener. Communication is successful when the speaker's message has been acknowledged by the listener sufficiently for the speaker to experience having successfully delivered the intended message. At each point in this process, the potential for miscommunication exists. The speaker's expression may be inarticulate, unclear or affected by emotion, physical illness, prejudice and lack of sophistication or other limitations.

Similarly, the listener's ability to hear and interpret the message may be impaired by parallel limitations. Also, the speaker or listener may incorrectly assume a context of understanding and appreciation for not only the words chosen, but their meaning to the speaker and listener. Thwarted, incomplete, or stifled communication is common in litigation. The mediator creates the possibility for successful communication through the mediation process by the use of effective listening.

Effective listening derives from the listener's commitment to receive the speaker's intended message, even if the expression of that message is muddled or incomplete. It involves the heart as well as the head; listening to what is not said; recognizing how communications are made, by whom, and from what positions, prejudices, points of view, and limitations communications originate. Effective listening also requires the listener to consciously recognize and be aware of his or her own limitations, prejudices, emotions, and reaction, and to take those into account in interpreting and translating what is being said.

One of the most powerful experiences a human being can enjoy is having his or her communication understood and received by another non-judgmental human being. This experience is at the heart of the success of the mediation process. The emotional release that results from a person successfully completing previously thwarted efforts at communication is often the catalyst, which allows parties to negotiate an acceptable settlement. Very often, meaningful negotiation does not occur without this emotional release.

Successful communication is a function of effective listening. The essence of effective listening is the listener's commitment to receive the speaker's intended message, even if the expression of that message is inadequate. The mediator generates the context for successful communication in the mediation process by his or her unqualified commitment to listen effectively.

APPENDIX II
The Mediator

In 1988, Steve asked me if I was familiar with the Peace Pilgrim. I had heard of it, but didn't know much about it. He explained that the Peace Pilgrim was a woman, who in her lifetime had abandoned personal possessions and walked over 25,000 miles for peace until her death in 1981. During 1987, Steve observed more and more the losses incurred by clients and others, due to endless legal fees from battles in the litigation process. He began to explore and study the principles offered by the Peace Pilgrim program, which could be applied to the legal profession. Steve would go on to become the founder of the attorney-mediator association, establishing mediation in the great state of Texas.

The "Spirit of Peace" Documentary, produced by Friends of Peace Pilgrim, included in one of their newsletters a segment entitled LAWYER'S COMMENTS IN THE SPIRIT OF PEACE ... Steve Brutsché, a lawyer and certified specialist in Dallas, Texas. It noted that Steve was inspired by the words of Peace Pilgrim to begin a program to use mediation for settling civil disputes. The documentary movie crew interviewed lawyers in Texas who are part of this mediation program. The following is a verbatim report of their taped words.

Lawyer #1: I think Steve was totally influenced by Peace Pilgrim. Everything else he read and studied was built on those same principles. I think it was his Bible, if you will— something he always went back to. And I think that Peace Pilgrim really affected him. I'm not sure the movement would have happened without the guidance Steve got from Peace Pilgrim. Because that was what inspired him to do everything else he did. His handing out Peace Pilgrim brochures was wonderful that Steve would hand out something like that. That was a pretty bold step in the dog eat dog litigation days we were in, in the late 80's.

Lawyer #2 – Steve Brutsché: What is missing in the practice of law for the vast majority of people is the sense that what they're doing contributes to something important. The paradigm for mediating is that you're peacemakers. There is a quality of doing good in mediating, of being a source of healing. Think "win-win" or "no deal." That's the rule of interpersonal relationships. Peace Pilgrim says that it's gotta be beneficial to everybody or it won't last.

Lawyer #3: Only HE (Steve) could look at a group of tenacious trial lawyers and say, "You've been greedy pigs, you sold out, for winning and for money, and that's not enough to sustain a life." And after 25,000 cases we have a steady 80% success rate regardless of who the mediator is. And that's important. Because the miracle is not in the persona of the mediator. It's in the process. It's based on universal principles that Peace Pilgrim enunciated that were not original with her. The basic underlying principle is that there is a spark of divine goodness in us all and that there is an abiding desire to seek and achieve peace and harmony.

Lawyer #4: He pulled out this little brochure and said, "You need this. You need to read this. This is everything you need to know." And he handed out the little Peace Pilgrim brochure.

In June 1990, the Texas Bar Journal published Steve's article "MEDIATION CROSS-EXAMINED". His closing paragraph was as follows: "Mediation is an idea whose time has come. It is here, it works, and it serves our clients. It is incumbent upon attorneys as the 'preeminent professional conflict managers' to utilize this effective method of dispute resolution." Pass the witness.

Steve was the founder and president of the Association of Attorney-Mediators. He trained advocates, the judiciary, and attorney-mediators in the mediation process. Both the Association of Attorney-Mediators and the American Arbitration Association have the honor of granting the "Steve Brutsché Award" to those persons who personify attorney dispute resolution for mediation and arbitration and for professional excellence in dispute resolution.

APPENDIX III
The Manipulator

From the records of the FSLIC:

In January, 1982 Don Dixon acquired over 90% of the outstanding stock of Vernon savings (Vernon). At that time, Vernon had total assets of $82.6 million, for branch offices and two subsidiaries.

In June 1982, the Federal Home Loan Bank Board (FHLBB) approved the transfer of Vernon stock by Dixon to Dondi Financial Corporation (DFC). Vernon was reorganized in May, 1983 as follows:

In simultaneous transactions, DFC exchanged the newly issued shares of DFC common stock for all of the outstanding capital stock of Dondi Group Inc., a Dixon controlled company, and then exchanged all of the newly acquired Dondi Group stock for newly issued Vernon common stock. As a result, Dondi Group, and its eight subsidiaries, became a wholly-owned subsidiary of Vernon. Based on this transaction, Vernon's reported net worth increased by more than $9.1 million, which represented the purported value of the non-cash contribution of Dondi Group.

Following Dixon's acquisition of Vernon, the deposits of Vernon grew from approximately $80 million in 1982 to nearly $1.6 billion in 1986. During the same period, the officers at Vernon Savings disregarded sound lending practices and conducted the real estate lending business of Vernon with the intent of maximizing fee income. They engaged in the following practices, among others:

Vernon focused on more risky commercial acquisition, development, and construction loans. By 1987, 80% to 85% of the Vernon loan portfolio consisted of ADC loans.

Vernon typically charged four points as the loan origination fee, although the industry standard was only two points. Vernon also typically charged one or two points as loan renewal fees every six months, although the industry standard was one or two points every 12 months. In addition, the interest rate charged by Vernon was higher than industry standards.

Vernon routinely extended additional credit to its troubled borrowers for the payment of past-due interest and for renewal loan fee charges, to prevent technical default on their loans.

Vernon frequently purchased profit participations from borrowers that did not have cash to pay interest or loan fee charges. Generally, the price paid by Vernon was based upon speculation rather than current, reliable appraisals or other information. Vernon generally reported these participations as immediate income.

Vernon sold loan participations to other lending institutions in an attempt to shield its rapid growth from examiners and to comply with legal restriction on growth rate. With respect to many of these loan participations, Vernon entered into contracts with the purchasing institution, whereby Vernon agreed to repurchase the participation in the event of default by the borrower. These contracts were not disclosed to either the examiners or the auditors of Vernon, and were not reflected as liabilities on the books and records of Vernon. The amount of loan participations, which were subject to these concealed buyback agreements and were not reported as liabilities by Vernon, exceeded $108,100,000 by March 1986.

Vernon continued to make payments to loan participants, even when the loan borrowers defaulted on loan interest payments to Vernon. This practice enabled Vernon to conceal from the loan participants the loan defaults, and to avoid the obligation to buy back the loan participations.

Borrowers from Vernon routinely funded their loan delinquency amounts by borrowing additional money from Vernon.

The officers of Vernon routinely changed the minutes of the Vernon Board of Directors meetings by deleting certain information and by adding other information, including approvals for new loans and loan extensions. The amended minutes were not presented or disclosed to the Board of Directors and did not accurately reflect the actions of the board.

The officers of Vernon routinely deleted from the monthly Vernon loan delinquency list, a sufficient number of delinquent loans, so that the total amount of reported delinquent loans would not exceed a designated amount. As many as 50% to

75% of the delinquent loans were typically deleted as a result of this process. The officers of Vernon presented the reduced, inaccurate delinquency list to the Vernon Board of Directors and regulatory examiners as the correct list.

The officers of Vernon, including Dixon, required borrowers to invest in entities and projects owned and controlled by those officers as a condition to Vernon loaning money to them. For example, officers required borrowers to invest in the yacht "High Spirits" as a condition of transacting business with Vernon.

With Vernon's consent, a cease-and-desist order was entered by the FHLBB on July 15, 1986. The order required Vernon to cease violating numerous federal regulations which prohibit certain lending practices, self-dealing, and improper financial accounting.

In September, 1986, the Texas Commissioner of Savings and Loan Associations placed his supervisory agent in Vernon's offices to oversee the operations of Vernon.

The financial statements of Vernon for the period ending November 30, 1986, prepared before a review of Vernon's loan files monitored by the supervisory agents, reported a negative net worth of over $17 million. This amount was an inaccurate overstatement of Vernon's true net worth by at least $300 million.

On January 22, 1987, the Board of Directors of Vernon approved an increase of $300,260,000 in loan-loss reserves for the period ending December 31, 1986. This adjustment was based upon a review of 58% of the loan balances existing as of June 30, 1986, and reflected loans which had been delinquent and substantially uncollectible for many months. Loan-loss reserves on the remaining 42% of the loan balances have not yet been established. Accordingly, the foregoing adjustment did not include any reserves against these remaining loan balances. Based in part upon this increase in loan-loss reserves, the financial statements of Vernon for the period ending December 31, 1986 reported a negative net worth of $350 million.

As of April, 1987, approximately 95% of Vernon's commercial loan portfolio was in default.

It was subsequently learned that Vernon maintained a fleet of five airplanes, including two jets, and employed six full-time pilots. From July 1983 to July 1986, Vernon incurred expenses of approximately $5,575,000 for the operation and maintenance of the aircraft, but received only $82,172 in income from the rental of the aircraft. Dixon and various officers of Vernon made numerous personal flights on Vernon aircraft.

On December 31, 1984, Vernon purchased a beach house on the Pacific coast in Delmar, California for approximately $2 million. Neither approval by the Board of Directors nor an independent appraisal was obtained in connection with the purchase. Dixon and his wife moved into the house in June 1985 and lived there rent free until the house was sold on June 2, 1986. Thereafter, he paid monthly rent to the subsequent owner of $7,100 per month. Vernon paid for the furnishings, improvements, and the Dixons' living expenses, which exceeded $308,400.

Vernon paid approximately $800,000 in total for these types of expenses. Vernon also paid over $900,000 for numerous works of art kept at the Delmar beach house.

Vernon paid more than $68,000 for personal travel expenses in connection with numerous trips to Europe by Dixon and his wife, and other officers.

In May 1985, Vernon, through its wholly-owned subsidiary Dondi Designs, expended approximately $489,000 for the purchase in England of furnishings for a personal residence owned by Dondi Associates Inc., a corporation wholly-owned by Dixon.

APPENDIX IV
The Pardon Request

I respectfully file this application for Presidential Pardon for the following reasons.

The first and foremost reason is that I have been encouraged to file this application for Presidential Pardon by persons who believe that such a pardon is really possible. These people are Dale V. Hogue, the Senior FBI agent who prosecuted my case at Vernon Savings and Loan and Robert Hauberg, Jr. and Steven P. Learned, who were the attorneys for the Department of Justice who prosecuted my case at Vernon Saving. In discussing the prospect of a Presidential Pardon with Special Agent Dale Hogue, I was asked to provide a letter for Steve and Robert that would help to update them as to what I have been doing for the past 15 years. I enclose a copy of this letter that I wrote to them last January as Exhibit "A". Also, I attach as Exhibit "B" a letter from Steven Learned, Attorney for the Department of Justice, stating his willingness to assist in this application for Presidential Pardon.

Second, I once again would like to become active in my community as a volunteer in various charitable programs, explore the possibility of running for a seat on the local school board, join the local Rotary Club, and expand my efforts of providing affordable housing to include the raising of funds from outside sources that will most certainly require detailed disclosures of my background. In my letter to Robert and Steve (Exhibit "A"), I describe my experience as a Summit County, Colorado School Board Member as an example of just how difficult it is to participate actively in community affairs when you carry the stigma of a felony conviction. I do understand that this application for Presidential Pardon is not for removal of my felony conviction, but for forgiveness, which would be very helpful in similar situations by reducing the stigma of my conviction.

I wish to do these things with the forgiveness of the President of the United States, so that I may make contribution of my time and effort in charitable, community activities without fear of embarrassment from my previous felony conviction. I enclose a copy of the newspaper article concerning the public embarrassment as a school board member as Exhibit "C." I also enclose as Exhibit "D" a page from an application form for volunteer work at Cook's Children's Hospital in Fort Worth, Texas reflecting disclosure of previous felony convictions and an article from the Wall Street Journal as Exhibit "E" discussing same. I also enclose as Exhibit "F" Parade Magazines cover concerning a call to volunteer service by President Bush.

Last, I have over the years tried to right the wrong that I caused at Vernon Savings and Loan through testifying for the United States Department of Justice and by giving speeches on the topic of ethics. For 14 years I have been the key witness for the Department of Justice, testifying numerous times in both criminal and civil cases. I am told by the Department of Justice that my cooperation and testimony have saved the Federal Government millions of dollars and countless hours of time.

Of my three Character Affidavits that are enclosed, one is from Jonathon Blacker who is the Department of Justice attorney that defended the Federal Government against a recent claim arising from a Vernon Savings and Loan matter, in which I was again the lead witness for the Government.

Over the years, I have given many speeches to colleges, universities, churches, trade schools, etc., regarding my experiences at Vernon Savings. These include: Southern Methodist University, University of North Texas, University of Texas at Arlington, University of Texas at Dallas, East Texas State University, Iowa State University, Texas Tech University, Stephen F. Austin University, Garland Community College-Arkansas, Texas Regional Junior College Administrators, Dallas and Denton Chapters of CPA's, Team Bank Executive Seminar, and others. My speech is entitled "(Un)Ethical Practices in Business and the Impact of Your Decisions on Your Career and Your Life". With the everyday news of corporate/financial fraud and deception, I know that I have a message that should again be heard, especially by those in college who will be our business leaders of the future. I often think about opening myself up and sharing my experiences again, but the thought of scandal and the impact on my family has kept me quiet. Having a Presidential Pardon would lessen the stigma of my felony conviction and would serve to propel me back to the podium.

Since the beginning weeks of the investigation of Vernon Savings and Loan, I have tried in every way possible to right my crime, my wrong, and to be a responsible, productive citizen. I sincerely regret that my actions, including my lack of proper action, caused problems, heartaches, and pain for others.

I must confess that the uncertainty of what this application will bring has caused me to take nearly a year to complete it. I respectfully submit this application and trust that it will be given genuine consideration. Thank you.

John Smith

www.ingramcontent.com/pod-product-compliance
Lightning Source LLC
Chambersburg PA
CBHW020613300426
44113CB00007B/626